Freak Show Without a Tent

Swimming with Piranhas,
Getting Stoned in Fiji,
and Other Family Vacations

By Nevin Martell

April - Let your Freak Fly!

ISBN: 978-0615889337

Published and distributed by
Possibilities Publishing
www.possibilitiespublishingcompany.com

Portions of *It Wasn't Like This the Last Time*
were originally published in *The Washington Post* in 2013.

For my family

What a long, strange, wonderful trip it's been

"A journey is a person in itself; no two are alike. And all plans, safeguards, policing, and coercion are fruitless. We find after years of struggle that we do not take a trip; a trip takes us."

John Steinbeck, *Travels With Charley: In Search of America*

Prologue

I have always found comfort in the steady drone of a jet's engines. Their thrumming white noise decompresses me as I head out on vacation, serves as a lullaby as I slip into sleep, and cradles me one last time as I return home.

This whooshing, whirring soundtrack accompanied our flight to the tropical getaway of Nevis. We were halfway there, soaring somewhere over the Caribbean Sea. Lunch had been served and I had eaten all of it. Every bite of rubbery chicken with glutinous cream sauce, tasteless steamed broccoli, and the freezer-burned salad drenched with chunky Thousand Island dressing, plus a square of chocolate cake that was equal parts sugared lard and cardboard. At the time, this mass-produced corporate fare seemed like a treat when compared to my mother's homespun cooking.

Though I was only six years old, I was already a seasoned traveler. My parents took me on my first trip shortly after I was born. We headed to Cognac, France, where they let me crawl through chateau hallways and eat French fare off their plates. Trips to Spain and Italy followed. Most recently, there had been a vacation to Bermuda, an experience that made me naively believe I knew all there was to know about island living.

To drive that point home to strangers on this trip to Nevis, I was wearing a Hawaiian shirt dotted with tiki gods and hula girls. Sunglasses with a black bridge and neon green temples hung jauntily at its V. Around my waist, a fanny pack was firmly strapped, chock-full of goodies from my mother.

Every time we took a trip that involved more than a couple hours in transit, Mom would curate care packages for my sister and me. To amuse myself, I began unpacking mine and carefully cataloging the contents on the tray table.

Four all-natural fruit leathers: one blackberry, one raspberry, and two strawberries.

Yellow crackers and spreadable orange cheese.

A small square paperback of *The Swiss Family Robinson*.

Explorer-themed playing cards.

Five dollars in spending money.

In other words, everything I could ever possibly want or need in the case of an emergency situation.

If we got stranded somewhere, like the Robinsons, I was certain that I could subsist on these supplies for three, if not four, months. I carefully repacked my survival kit and strapped my fanny pack back on, giving the belt an extra tug to ensure it was snugly attached.

Leaning across my sleeping younger sister Josephine, I waved a hand at my parents to get their attention. My mother was reading, while my father nursed his second scotch on the rocks and contemplated the seat back in front of him. His gaze didn't shift; she turned immediately.

"Thanks, Mom. Awesome stuff," I stage whispered across Jo.

She lowered her book. "I'm glad you like it. Don't eat everything before we get there; space it out."

I nodded vigorously. She clearly didn't know I was in survivalist mode. Anyway, there were more important issues to be addressed.

"I have to go to the bathroom."

Craning her neck toward the back of the plane, she nodded. "All right. No one's in line. Be quick about it."

She returned to her paperback, while I unclicked my seatbelt and shimmied into the aisle. The sign in the slot on the door read "vacant," so I twisted the handle and popped in. When you use a plane bathroom accompanied by a full-sized adult, who made sure you wiped completely and didn't pee on the lid, things are pretty cramped. All alone, it felt almost spacious. I could just see the top of my head and thick Coke-bottle glasses in the mirror above the sink. When I sat down on the toilet and stretched out my legs, they didn't even touch the door.

Sitting back, I let my eyes close as I thought about the relaxing vacation ahead of us. White sand beaches, warm waters to snorkel in, and plenty of virgin piña coladas. From everything Dad had been telling us for the last couple of months at dinner, Nevis was paradise.

Imagining I was in a lounge chair, I leaned back farther. I could almost feel the sun's rays warming my face, hear the waves lapping at the shoreline, and smell the thick layer of maximum SPF suntan lotion that my mother would inevitably coat me with several times a day. Island living, here I come!

Thirsting from my vision, I reached over in my daydream to grab the glass adorned with a blue plastic monkey and a paper umbrella on the ground beside me. My hand was just about to grasp it when suddenly the weirdest thing happened – I started to slowly slide forward off my chair away from it.

Hunh?

You're supposed to have complete control in daydreams. Nightmares when you're asleep are a different matter entirely – and I'd had a few of those over the years – but artistic autonomy was the great part about fantasizing when you're awake.

What the hell?

My eyes flipped open and I immediately knew that something was very, very wrong. The bathroom was at an angle that favored the earth rather than the horizon. Like we were landing. One small problem: We weren't set to hit the tarmac for more than an hour.

Ding! The "fasten seat belts" light came on.

As if that wasn't unreassuring enough, the cabin took on an even more drastic downward angle.

Uh-oh. This was *not* good.

I wasn't the only person on the plane to feel this way about our unexpected pitch toward terra firma. My fellow passengers celebrated this new trajectory by starting to scream. These were not the cries of overly excited vacationers – these sounded scared and helpless. Not that mine sounded any less scared or helpless as I filled the space of the cramped lavatory with all that my little lungs had to give. As if to complement this discord, the reassuring drone of the engines was suddenly replaced by a high-pitched mechanical wail.

Bracing myself on the sides of the bathroom, which suddenly felt like the smallest, most claustrophobic room in the world – just about the size of a coffin – I found myself at odds. On the one hand, dignity and my mother's upbringing required that I pull up my shorts before I presented myself publicly. On the other, my instincts were telling me to get the hell out of this airborne sarcophagus as quickly as possible.

Why had Mother Nature called? If only I was back in my seat. Not only did it come equipped with a seatbelt and a cushion that doubled as a life preserver, but it was also next to my mother. There was no doubt in my mind that she would be able to protect me from whatever came next. Another thing was certain: She had not provisioned my fanny pack with this particular situation in mind, unless I had somehow missed a miniature parachute in my survey.

I was diverted from my contemplation when the screams outside the door became more frantic. Dull thumps, heavy thuds, and sharp thwacks punctuated the human hysteria.

To add one last unnerving component to the equation, an air mask suddenly dropped down from the ceiling above me. I instinctively reached up for it, forgetting that both arms were required for my human brace to work.

I tumbled forward, landing against the door. My shoulder flashed with a sharp pain, but it didn't seem to matter in light of the present circumstances. What's a little ding when you might die?

The speaker on the ceiling boomed to life for a terse, terrifying three-word announcement.

"Fasten your seatbelts." The "s" hadn't finished being pronounced when the voice clicked off.

I took stock of my options. I was at a 45-degree angle and standing, as if leaning into hurricane grade winds. If I could get out of what was looking more and more like my gravesite, I might be able to get back to my seat.

Hastily, I pulled up my shorts. Sliding back the lock, I turned the handle slowly with one hand and gripped the frame as best I could with the other. I half swung, half fell forward as the door opened outward. Suddenly, the shouting was louder – a jumble of voices and languages. Through it all, I thought I could hear my mother screaming my name.

The scene was abject chaos. People were in their seats, but clutching the armrests, hugging their knees with their head pointed to the floor or still grasping above themselves for an elusive air mask. Plastic cups, newspapers, and pillows tumbled down the aisle.

My seat was halfway back up the plane – downhill and through all that mayhem. I stood there for a second, clutching the seatback in front of me, unsure of how to proceed.

That's when a stewardess in the last row saw me, wrapped her arm around my waist, and yanked me into her lap.

"Got you."

I could only nod. I could feel her shaking beneath me, though I couldn't tell if it was the bone-rattling vibrations of the plane or her own fear.

She pulled down an air mask and slipped the elastic loops around my head. As soon as the mask covered my mouth, I let out a huge breath that I hadn't realized I had been holding. Then my breaths came quickly, in short, sharp bursts.

This could be it. The grand finale. That moment in the play when the curtains close but the houselights are still dark. The end.

I had a very vague sense of death. The only one I had experienced was when our dog P2 died unexpectedly, which was devastating. His passing was like losing a friend, and I had been inconsolable for days.

I wondered briefly who would cry for me. Definitely Gramma and Grampa. My cousins, I hoped. Probably some of our neighbors. Maybe a few of the kids in my class at school. Unfortunately, my parents and sister wouldn't be there to mourn. A short list, no matter how you looked at it.

My breaths were coming quicker. It was strange though – the din was getting quieter. In fact, if you subtracted the banshee wail of the engines and the creaking of the plane's stressed hull, it was almost silent. Most of the yells had stopped, as people had turned from loud shrieking to silent prayers. Our family didn't go to church, so I was unclear of what you said or whom you directed it to in this kind of situation. So I turned from God and the heavenly host above to the next highest-ranking saint that I knew: Saint Nick.

In my head, I penned a quick letter.

Dear Santa,

I'd very much like to spend this Christmas alive with my family. Please. I'll leave out a million cookies for you and a bunch of carrot sticks for the reindeer. I'll do all my chores, behave at the dinner table, and be really nice to Jo. She can even play with my Star Wars *figures whenever she wants. Just please, please, please help me right now.*

I squeezed my eyes shut, hung on to the stewardess, and prayed with all my heart to the patron saint of the North Pole. Don't let me join the family dog just yet!

Good old Saint Nick must have been monitoring his telepathic mailbox at that moment.

Suddenly and jarringly, the plane's heading started to turn upward.

It wasn't a graceful, balletic movement. The engines strained hard, fighting to pull us out of our tragic trajectory toward terra firma.

The g-forces pushed me back against the stewardess and her into the seat. My already whitened knuckles turned almost translucent as my hand clutched the top of hers. I could feel tears running down my face, though I wasn't sure when I started crying. Come on, Santa, please don't fail me now!

Slowly, surely, the jet found its balance point and resumed a flat flight path. Inquisitive cries rippled through the cabin. I let my grip on the stewardess's hand relax ever so slightly.

The speaker above me crackled to life. "Hello, folks, this is the captain. Everything is okay."

A collective sigh of relief rushed through the space. There were cheers mixed with the sound of sobbing, including my wracked breaths. I could feel the stewardess unwind beneath me, almost melting into her seat with relief.

"We lost pressure in the cabin," the captain continued. "Due to the uncontrolled decompression, we had to deploy the oxygen masks and immediately descend to 8,000 feet or else there could have been dire consequences for all of us. Thankfully, that didn't happen."

He paused for a second, then continued, "We'll be diverting to San Juan, Puerto Rico, to switch planes. In the meantime, the stewardesses will be coming around with the drink carts in a few minutes. Get whatever you want – it's all on the house."

That stopped most of the crying instantaneously. A Hollywood-worthy huzzah went up from the passengers. There was clapping, high fiving, and hugging everywhere. I wasn't sure if it was because everyone was happy to be alive or simply because they were getting free cocktails.

My mother rushed over through the celebrations. She crouched in the aisle, a look of concern splashed across her usually smiling face.

"Are you okay?"

I managed a nod as I buried my head in her shoulder. Hugging me close, she murmured, "I'm sorry I wasn't there."

I didn't care. I was just happy to be alive and back in her protective custody.

After thanking the stewardess over and over, until she reminded us that there was a plane full of passengers who were expecting complimentary cocktails, we headed back to rejoin the rest of the family. Reaching our row, I clambered into my seat to find my sister and father staring at me like I had just returned from a vacation that they clearly worried might have been permanent.

"Don't worry. I'm okay," I reassured them, settling in and fastening my seatbelt.

Dad smiled widely. It was a grin I would come to associate with risks being taken without the realization that there were potential downsides.

"Pretty exciting way to start our vacation, right?" he said in what sounded like a genuinely enthusiastic tone.

Even then, when I was so young and barely knew better about most things, I knew that near-death experiences shouldn't be considered exciting. They should be studiously avoided at all costs. You don't seek out heart-stopping thrills like that - you sprint in the opposite direction from them.

I wanted to correct my father, but I couldn't. I just didn't have the heart. Who was I to tell him that his glass was half empty when he was convinced it was brimming full?

"Definitely, Dad," I agreed, not realizing this was just the beginning.

Real Men Wear Bark Penis Sheaths

[Vanuatu 1986, Age 12]

Pan Am used to give out winged pins to young passengers, American Airlines passed out decks of cards, and Delta provided first-class flyers with a shoehorn if they were having a problem with their loafers. However, as I stepped onto the Air Fiji flight heading to Vanuatu in the South Pacific, a beaming stewardess in a tight-fitting polyester skirt and blazer greeted me with a lei of off-white shells.

"Welcome aboard," she said as she slipped it around my neck.

I didn't know the proper response, so I half-bowed back like I'd recently seen Daniel-san do in *The Karate Kid.* Shuffling past her down the aisle, my latest accessory delicately clinking like a New Age wind chime, I couldn't help but grin. No more chores, no more homework, and no more boring routine. We were headed to paradise! I could only hope that this flight was less eventful than our trip to Nevis.

Our destination was the capital city of Port Vila on Efate, one of more than 80 islands that make up the Republic of Vanuatu. It would have been an odd choice to most vacationers, who usually only debated whether to go to Disney World or Club Med. Not us. My father burned with an insatiable wanderlust, compelling him to pick the most out-of-the-way places in the world for our trips.

Unlike many of the families I knew growing up in western New York and then eastern Pennsylvania, ours was not bound by the usual conventions. Dad had owned Martell's, a successful Manhattan restaurant, for well over two decades. However, when he sold it in 1985, he was suddenly afforded freedom and the funds to explore the world.

The family didn't hold him back from his dreams of exploring the lesser-known corners of the planet. Josephine and I could easily be taken out of school for substantial stretches or simply transferred into new ones. Not yet 40, my mother was unattached to a professional career, though taking care of the three of us was undoubtedly a full-time job with plenty of overtime and not enough gratitude from her charges.

Without strong ties keeping them held down, my parents had moved us to New Zealand on my 11th birthday, which I hope will always rank as my least-attended birthday party ever. Both of them had fond memories of traipsing through the Land of the Long White Cloud on their honeymoon. However, that had been over a decade ago.

They hadn't done much research before we'd arrived in New Zealand, so we started out living in Russell, a rustic fishing town on the northern tip of the North Island. That decision turned out to be the equivalent of deciding you're going to move to America and randomly picking Podunk, Idaho, as your new hometown. Ultimately, we ended up in Nelson, at the uppermost end of the South Island, a more modernized seaport that felt not unlike a small city in the Pacific Northwest.

Our new address was a perfect base of operations for my father's plans to practically retrace Captain Cook's travels through the South Pacific. That was how we had ended up heading to Vanuatu. Though Dad had only bought the country's guidebook in the airport on the day that we departed, he had been talking about the potential adventures that lay ahead for weeks beforehand. There was no doubt that something special was in store for us, though none of us really knew what that might be.

When we touched down on Efate and the flight crew opened the door, the cabin flooded with moist tropical air. I breathed in deeply, adjusted my shell necklace, and double-checked that my fanny pack was fastened tightly about my waist. Bring on the paradise! As I disembarked, I made sure to bow to every member of the crew I encountered. No one would ever be able to accuse me of being an impolite out-of-towner.

Driving through Port Vila a short while later, the rays of the unrelenting South Pacific sun pried open my travel-bleary eyes. The city still felt like a colonial outpost; there were reminders of times past everywhere you looked. We passed a couple 19th-century mansions that still clung to their majesty, even as they slowly succumbed to the ravages of time, hurricanes, and the brutal decaying effects of salt air.

Vanuatuans hung out in front of small stores chatting and enjoying cold beers in the hot afternoon. As we zipped by an open-air market, the rich scent of coconut oil mixed with fresh fish, ripened pineapple, and a faint undercurrent of diesel to create an intoxicatingly exotic aroma. A few tourists dotted the sidewalks, garish in their big sun hats, oversized sunglasses, and brightly colored bathing suits.

Unfortunately, our hotel was more North America than South Pacific, which didn't sit well with my father. "Looks like Cleveland," he muttered.

I had never been to Cleveland, but I knew it wasn't a compliment.

"Don't worry," he needlessly continued. "We'll get out to the *real* Vanuatu soon enough."

I didn't quite understand what wasn't real about the Vanuatu I was standing in just then. This all seemed very real to me.

My sister and I had barely put our bags down and fought over who would sleep in which bed – I ended up in the one by the balcony, which I thought was the nicer option – before Dad appeared in the doorway of our room.

"Come on, kids. Let's go exploring."

He sounded like a children's television show host who really loved his job. This was probably at least partly because his bartender-turned-restaurateur-turned-retiree career arc allowed him to never grow up. You can't argue with such youthful enthusiasm, even when the speaker was nearly 60 years old. I was fried, but I still found it impossible to say no.

"Should be fun," I half-heartedly replied, wondering if it was possible to maybe, just maybe, squeeze in a quick nap before we headed out.

Jo looked up from her suitcase to deliver a deadpan, "Totally," before returning to her unpacking.

Dad apparently didn't notice our marked lack of energy and enthusiasm, or just chose to ignore it. "This is going to be an adventure! And who knows where it's going to take us?"

"Who knows?" I echoed tentatively with a weak smile. "Into the great unknown. Right, Dad?"

He came over to give me a manly half-hug across the shoulders. "Thatta boy. All right, I've got to get my camera gear together."

Disappearing as abruptly as he had arrived, he left us to prepare ourselves for our inaugural survey of Port Vila. Always the pragmatist, I strapped on my fanny pack and filled it with a couple of packages of cheese and crackers, a box of raisins, sun block, and a pocket-sized copy of *Robinson Crusoe*.

"Come on, Jo. Let's get down there before he has a conniption."

"Why is he being such a dick-tater?" she enunciated fiercely.

"Who cares? I'm hungry."

"Yeah, yeah, yeah." Jo snapped on her own turquoise fanny pack across her travel-rumpled Guatemalan dress and pushed me towards the door. "Move it, junior dick-tater."

When we met my parents in the lobby, it looked like a reunion of two totally different families. While Jo and I had barely been able to get ourselves together, Mom and Dad had somehow transformed themselves into dead ringers for the stars of *Romancing the Stone*. My mother's hair was pulled back into a loose ponytail, and she was wearing a lavender top with embroidered edging. Dad sported khaki shorts and a loose white linen shirt unbuttoned halfway, subjecting every passerby to an eyeful of his graying chest hair.

Dad quickly formed a strong opinion about our more rustic

traveling getup. "You guys could be Lois and Clark," he quipped.

"Who are you then? Christopher Dumbass?" Jo shot back.

"Or Vasco da Asso," I added helpfully, figuring that it was always best to redirect Jo's ire in an alternate direction than my own.

Mom wasn't amused with the way the conversation was heading. "No Dumbass. No Asso. Don't worry; you both look very cute."

She shot my father a look to keep him from disagreeing with her; he just shrugged. "I know everyone is a little worn out," she said diplomatically. "Let's stop bickering and get a bite to eat."

If there was one thing that could always put an end to arguments in our family, it was food. Forming up ranks, we headed outside. Walking down the street perked me up and made me realize that my belly was feeling more than a little empty. I could have eaten the cheese and crackers or the raisins in my fanny pack, but I was seasoned enough to know that you never eat your supplies on the first day. Just look at what happened to the Donner Party – worst party ever.

A few blocks from the hotel, my nose caught the scent of a deep fryer working overtime. The source of the smell was Bloody Mary's Restaurant, which advertised fish 'n' chips, milkshakes, burgers, and "island fare." The promise of fatty fast food reminded me of the States, so it was reassuring to see this little slice of wannabe Americana in the faraway heart of Melanesia.

"What if we stop here?" I suggested, nudging my sister.

Jo took my lead and rolled out her sad puppy eyes. "Yeah, I'm starving, Dad."

My father hemmed and hawed for a second. Clearly, he wanted to keep going and canvass the entire town before coming to a dining decision, but he was swayed by our pitiful looks.

"I guess we could try it," he conceded.

"Mmm, mango milkshakes," my mother cooed as we steered into the shade of the restaurant's patio and sat down in sun-bleached plastic chairs at a small table with a red-and-white-checkered tablecloth. A half-filled ketchup bottle and an old mayonnaise jar brimming with homemade hot sauce sat at its center. The waiter brought over menus, but little did he know that he was wasting time and energy. One of the rules in my father's travel book was that menus are for stick-in-the-muds.

Without even glancing at the options, Dad asked, "Do you have any specials?"

The waiter was clearly thrilled. "An adventurous eater. How wonderful."

My father preened and puffed out his chest as if he'd just been awarded a gold medal in the Olympics.

"Christopher Dumbass," my sister whispered out of the side of her mouth. I nodded, coughing my laughter into the napkin.

"Maybe you'd like to try the Millionaire's Salad?" the waiter inquired.

"What's that?" My father was clearly intrigued; so was I.

"We shred up the whole heart of a coconut palm," the waiter said, making slicing motions with his hands. "Since we're taking the tree's heart, we kill the entire palm just to make the salad. We call it the Millionaire's Salad because it's the most expensive item on the menu." He chuckled loudly at his own joke.

My father looked impressed by the proposition, but Jo was horrified. "Don't kill the tree, Dad," she pleaded. "Would you chop down a maple tree just to get a jug of syrup? I bet you wouldn't."

Dad was torn. He looked between the expectant waiter, who was offering a taste of the *real* Vanuatu that he yearned to experience, and his daughter, who would pester him for the rest of the trip for being a tree-killing monster.

The waiter tried to tip the scales in his favor. "If you are interested, sir, I can have them go cut down the tree right now."

Luckily for the poor palm on the chopping block, my mother stepped in with a pragmatic suggestion. "This sounds like it might take a long time, honey. Wouldn't it be more fun to be out exploring the island instead?"

Dad nodded. "You're right, dear." He turned back to the waiter. "I'll take the coconut crab and a gin and tonic."

Jo and I exchanged relieved glances as we each ordered fried poulet fish with French fries and virgin piña coladas; my mother opted to try a vegetarian sampler platter with taro and yams, and a glass of water.

As the waiter shuffled back to the kitchen with a defeated slump to his shoulders, my mother got out the guidebook and my father got that fanatical look in his eyes again.

"There's all sorts of stuff we can do," he told us gleefully, like a kid explaining the possibilities at an amusement park. I was pretty sure he'd barely read the guidebook that he had purchased just a few hours earlier, and surmised that Dad was flying by the seat of his pants. It was a strategy that would become his hallmark in years to come.

"There's a factory here that makes buttons out of shells. I'd like to check that out," my mother said.

"Maybe," my dad hemmed, but I could tell that a visit to the button plant was not on his ideal agenda. Not *real* or exciting enough.

"Oh, look at this, there's a glass-bottomed boat tour, too," my mother continued, valiantly struggling to mold this into a trip the rest of us might actually enjoy.

Dad decided to draw a line in the proverbial sand, reminding me that we hadn't even had a chance to see a beach yet, despite the fact that we were on an island in the South Pacific.

"Alison, we should really be considering the big-picture elements of the trip."

"You can also take a tour of the Mr. Juicy soda factory," Mom added, as if she hadn't heard him. "That might be fun for the kids."

My father looked even more crestfallen at this idea, but I was totally on board. Considering how carefully Mom regulated our sugar intake – having a super sweet piña colada was a vacation-only special treat – going to the source where high-fructose corn syrup-based beverages were made was almost better than Halloween treat bags, Christmas stockings, and Easter baskets combined.

"That sounds very cool," I chirped, my excitement betraying any attempt to sound nonchalant. As misfortune would have it, nobody was listening to me.

None of these options were sitting well with my father. "Let me see that, Alison," he bothered to ask as he all but lunged across the table to rip the guidebook from my mother's hands. He flipped through it with a quiet desperation until he finally alighted on a page that seemed to buoy his spirits.

"Ah, look here." He tapped the page. "There's a national cultural center right here in Port Vila. That would be the best place to start."

He put down the book with a satisfied smile that meant that our plans had been made. A cultural center? That sounded incredibly boring. The name itself held all the glamour of phrases like "agricultural college" and "home economics." It certainly didn't sound like the kind of place where you found an exciting adventure or the *real* Vanuatu.

* * * * *

Despite my misgivings, we found ourselves walking up to the Vanuatu Cultural Center and National Museum the next morning. I was instantly uninterested in the building itself and what it might hold when I saw the giant cauldron sitting out front. According to the weatherworn placard, it had once been used to boil visiting missionaries alive. The short paragraph was unclear about whether the tradition still thrived, which was unsettling.

As I stared into the black iron depths, I wondered what it must have felt like to be cooked to death. Being routinely forced to take a bath in a tub full of scalding hot water by my mother was bad enough, but at least she wasn't planning to eat me alive after I cleaned behind my ears. Clearly a trip to the cauldron was to be avoided at all costs.

Inside the center, there were more signs that foreigners hadn't always been welcomed with seashell necklaces and promises of paradise. A giant glass case displayed an astonishing array of hand-carved spears, cudgels, and war hammers (maybe to "help" any missionaries who didn't like the looks of the cauldron). This was far more interesting than I had anticipated. I kept my fingers crossed that there was a gift shop, where I might be able to buy some replicas of this weaponry to keep my sister in line.

Farther down the hall there was a series of wooden canoes, each hewn out of a single tree by a lone craftsman. Having barely assembled a beyond-rudimentary toy racing-car kit with my father for my Cub Scouts' Pinewood Derby, I couldn't begin to fathom the skill and patience required to build such a vessel. As we were all taking in the handiwork, a thin man with too much nervous energy, a sweat-spotted blue *guayabera* shirt often favored by Cuban barbers, and a graying, pointed goatee came up to us.

"Are you folks enjoying yourselves?" He grinned, not unlike how I imagined a local addressed a missionary who was about to become the main course.

"Oh, yes, this is very interesting," my mother graciously responded as she moved on to the next case of artifacts, hoping to sidestep an interaction with this peculiar character.

Dad couldn't pass up the opportunity to connect with a local and extended his hand. "I'm Ralph. This is my wife Alison and our two children, Nevin and Josephine."

"I'm Kirk Huffman," the man replied as he wrung my father's

hand with the kind of enthusiasm usually reserved for Stanley meeting Livingstone for the first time. "I'm the curator here."

"What are the chances?" my father exclaimed excitedly, half-turning to us, hoping some eager looks would materialize on our faces. "We came here to try to figure out what to do on our trip. I bet you've got your finger on the pulse."

Huffman smiled. "You're lucky; the vines are their most elastic at this time of year."

I was still staring at him with a "What the hell are you talking about, crazy man?" look on my face when my father dived into the breach.

"Vines?" he asked uncertainly. "Like the plant?"

"Come into my office and I'll tell you more."

Huffman ushered us all into an overcrowded room with piles of academic books, old magazines, and loosely arranged papers cluttering every possible surface. Small wooden statuettes, half-full Mr. Juicy bottles, and dusty shards of pottery punctuated the chaos. There was nowhere to sit, so we all stood awkwardly, wondering if we were going to accidentally break some priceless ancient artifact.

For the next hour, as we grew hotter, more cramped, and more uncomfortable, Huffman regaled us with stories about *naghol*, better known as land diving to Westerners. Every spring on nearby Pentecost Island, divers jumped off manmade wooden towers in the middle of the jungle with nothing but the aforementioned – and not-so-sturdy-sounding – vines strapped to their ankles.

It's basically bungee jumping minus the safety harness and the multimillion-dollar insurance policy, but it's no sport.

While *naghol* is a rite of manhood for young jumpers, the whole ceremony serves as a fertility ritual that ensures that tribes enjoy bountiful yam harvests. To me, it sounded like the most insane way to ask God a favor, a needlessly dangerous way to prove you had some *cojones*, and a bizarre way to pass an afternoon. However, to my father it was that really *real* experience that he'd been seeking.

"Does that sound like fun or what?" he crowed as we walked out of the cultural center, a reservation booked out to Pentecost the next day with the help of his new friend.

I didn't even know the words to a dinnertime grace, so I had a hard time comprehending the faith required to trust my life to a rickety tower and some flimsy jungle creepers. Though my fingers were tightly crossed that we didn't meet anyone with a cauldron, I was excited about the trip.

This would truly be an adventure. We were going to see a ceremony that had been practiced for hundreds of years. It would be like stepping into a time machine and whizzing back to the primitive age before telephones, Saturday morning cartoons, and cheese that came in aerosol cans. Suddenly our family vacation was on a Jules Verne-styled quest of epic proportions.

The next morning, we were up at five o'clock to get to the airport for our day trip. As we waited in the hotel lobby for my sister to come down, I saw a postcard about land diving in the gift shop. Next to a picture of a little lad in mid-fall, a small blurb explained, "Young boys follow trustingly in their fathers' footsteps to early learn this spectacular feat." I laughed out loud. If Dad ever asked me to jump off a tower to make sure everyone had their daily allowance of carbs, I'd head out the door to start my career as a professional hobo. These Vanuatuans were made of strong stuff!

When we got to the airport, I learned that Vanuatuans thrived on uncertainty and danger at every turn. The plane we were taking to Pentecost was a patched, re-patched, and patched again single-engine Cessna that had probably been in service since it came off the assembly line in the early '50's. Worse yet, it looked like the mechanic didn't have much of a budget for repairs. Duct tape was used to cover holes and brace the key junctures where the wing struts attached to the plane.

"Don't worry, it's stronger than steel," the expat American pilot reassured us with an easygoing grin that I prayed wasn't enhanced by a string of hair-of-the-dog beers in the airport bar.

As we walked up to what I was certain would be our collective coffin, my father inspected the repair work. "That stuff is a miracle," he nodded sagely. "You can use duct tape for anything."

Christopher Dumbass, indeed. Suddenly, I wasn't so excited. The only miracle I could see happening was if we survived this mockery of aeronautical engineering. Watching other people fall out of the sky was one thing; falling out of the sky in a duct-taped casket was another thing. But we didn't have a chance to debate our chances of survival before the pilot fired up the engine, cutting off any debate and sending us past the point of no return.

"Strap yourselves in," our Grim Reaper yelled over the tumult, but he didn't need to prompt us. We would have put on parachutes, helmets, and life preservers, if only they were available.

Taxiing to the end of the strip, he turned the plane into the wind and away from the sun. As he gunned the engine, I gripped my armrest – only to have it come away in my hand, trailing a bit of silvery gray tape. So much for the miracle of duct tape!

Squeezing my eyes tight, I tried to drown out the din. Every part of the plane was shaking, rattling, and clanking, producing a most ominous dissonance that reminded me of our midair disaster on the way to Nevis. In an unexpected moment of clarity, I suddenly realized that I had stopped breathing and was holding in the air. I hoped it wasn't my last breath. The noise increased like someone was cranking the volume knob far past the max.

Suddenly, the noise subsided dramatically and the sound became more of a drone than a wail. I slowly cracked open my eyes, peeking through my drawn lashes like a lion suspiciously searching the savannah for hunters. Sky, beautiful blue sky, stretched out before us, dotted with gargantuan clouds hewn into floating Arctic icebergs. Below us, the sun glinted off the ocean, creating an endless stream of sparkles that stretched to the horizon.

A few minutes later, we passed close to the neighboring island of Ambrym, where a heavy mist shrouded the volcano rising up at its center. It was one of those definitively primordial vistas that seemed to make you forget that you were living in the 20th century.

Looking down, I imagined peering through the patchwork of jade, chartreuse, and emerald foliage to discover a prehistoric world below. Dinosaurs stalked through the forest, giant kaleidoscopic butterflies flitted through the muggy air, and white-faced monkeys swung between the trees.

Quickly we passed over this lost world and soon Pentecost came into view. I looked around vainly for a landing strip, but all I could see was a long mucky meadow near the coast.

As if he was reading my mind, the pilot yelled back, "It doesn't look like LaGuardia, but it does the trick. I just hope they keep the goats off the runway this time."

I tightened my seatbelt and wondered if the plane came with airbags. Not that it mattered; they'd probably be made of duct tape anyway.

Crap.

Well, it's been fun.

The pilot banked sharply and nosed the plane toward the ground. Crosswinds buffeted the Cessna, and it shook violently. I looked out the window at the duct tape, wondering just how strong it really was. We were in an angled dive; the earth was rushing up at us. This time, I kept my eyes open, but only because I was too petrified to close them.

Why did I always get on the doomed flights? It's like Dad only knew how to buy one-way tickets to hell.

Then, suddenly, the pilot leveled out and touched down with a lightness that defied all logic and expectation. The sound of mud slapping against the undercarriage and the bleating of the goats mixing with the guttural roar of the plane covered my explosive sigh of relief as we came to a stop.

We disembarked as a pair of dirt-encrusted jeeps pulled up and two men got out. Our pilot greeted the drivers and began unloading boxes of food and bags of mail, which were quickly packed into the backs of the jeeps. Once this was done, one of the drivers came over to us. He was dressed in a set of faded standard-issue olive cargo pants and a shirt that claimed his last name was Miller and his rank was that of a colonel, but I was pretty certain that he never spent a day of his life in the service.

"I'm Nicholas, your guide," he told us in heavily accented, clipped English. "Welcome to Pentecost Island. This is only the third year we are allowing tourists to come here, so you are some of the first outsiders to ever witness the *naghol*."

Collectively, we gave a very impressed-sounding "oooh." It looked like Dad had scored the authentic Vanuatuan experience for which he had been searching.

We were so impressed by this turn of events that we were oblivious to another single-engine plane until it buzzed overhead, preparing to touch down. We watched as it looped around before it cut its own V through the sludge, scattering goats in the process. It pulled up a few feet away, whipping us with the sharp breeze of the propeller. The pilot hadn't even had a chance to cut the engine before the plane's door opened and four men jumped out like they were a Special Forces unit.

"Film crew," Nicholas informed us knowingly as he gave them a familiar wave. "They're making a movie about the *naghol*."

These filmmakers defied my expectations of Hollywood big shots. Instead of channeling the svelte style of Rodeo Drive, these guys preferred a more rough and rugged aesthetic. Clad in well-worn jungle khakis and dirty hiking boots, they all boasted a few days' worth of unshaven scruff. They looked more like adventurers searching for cities of lost gold rather than Spielberg wannabes. They certainly weren't searching for a pale-skinned family of four. After giving us a cursory glance and a perfunctory greeting, they piled into the second jeep and zoomed off.

We were on a tight schedule on Pentecost; there was just enough time to watch the ceremony before we'd be making a mad dash to get back to the plane. There were no hotels on the island, and overnight stays were prohibited. And since there was no proper airport – which meant there was no air traffic control, no homing beacon, and no gift shop where you could buy land-diver action figures or a "Land Diving Is De-Vine" bumper sticker – the pilot could only land during full daylight and in good weather. Even a landing in the evening or during a light shower would be suicidal, so the pilot stressed the importance of making it back to the landing strip by four o'clock.

"Pentecost can be a really dangerous place, so you don't want to spend the night." He gave a wave. "Did you see that cauldron they have in front of the cultural center? They have one here that's for the guests."

With that disturbing thought in mind, we turned our attention to our transportation for the next stage of our journey. Like the beat-up plane we had arrived in, this jeep had seen better days. Originally standard Army green when it was airdropped in during the Second World War, it was now bleached to a light olive and caked with mud. As my observant father cheerfully pointed out, duct tape covered several large rust holes near the jeep's undercarriage.

"If this repair work is as sturdy as that plane we came in on, we're in luck," he declared without a trace of irony.

My mother wasn't convinced. "Make sure you fasten your seatbelts, and no horsing around."

The front passenger seat was the only one with a working seatbelt, so my sister and I squeezed in together and secured ourselves. Nicholas jumped in and fired up the jeep, whose engine roared to life with encouraging energy. We headed down the muddy track alongside the clearing till we reached an even muddier dirt road wending its way into the jungle. It was loud with the wind rushing in and the engine straining to carry us across the arduous landscape, so we couldn't hear one another speak. This didn't stop Nicholas, who kept talking at us, his thickly accented English coming through in little bits and pieces that made no sense whatsoever.

"Long time…they died…Happy Meal…John Wayne."

"Yeah. Totally," Jo responded, displaying her remarkable ability to convince adults that she was both listening and caring about what they were saying while actually doing neither.

Frankly, we were both more interested in what was going on outside the vehicle than in it. We were fascinated by the passing scenery – a cacophony of greens and browns spotted with the bright flashes of colorful flowers that echoed a Jackson Pollock painting. Palm trees grew everywhere, their fronds hanging over the road and their upper reaches full of green coconuts.

After 10 minutes of bumping along the crude road, we came to small village made up of a couple dozen thatched huts arranged in a rough circle. Nicholas jumped out and started unloading some crates from the back, waving over a few men to retrieve what he was leaving. The sound of the jeep engine called everyone like a giant doorbell, so people started to pile out of their huts or emerge from deeper in the encampment.

Everyone was clearly intrigued by the four foreigners because a small crescent quickly formed around the jeep. Some of the mahogany-skinned locals politely pretended to talk to Nicholas while glancing at us out of the corners of their eyes, but most of them spared the pretense and just stared at us with open curiosity.

I was just as fascinated by them. The men were dressed in nothing more than hand-woven bark penis sheaths, which the guidebook had indicated were called *nambas*. They wore a woven black belt just above their hips, which attached to the sheath and yanked their penises upward in a way that looked so profoundly painful that I caught myself unconsciously clenching my legs together. The women had an easier time of it and were topless, their breasts hanging down toward their tan grass skirts. Smiling children dressed in first-world thrift-store wear – ratty T-shirts and frayed athletic shorts – ran among them. The island throng was filled out with chickens and the occasional tusked pig.

"What are we supposed to say?" I asked my sister as several of the children gathered together and started toward our side of the car in an energetic cluster bubbling over with chattering and hand waving.

Josephine shrugged. "I dunno. Maybe find out if we can play with the chickens?"

I wasn't sold on this fowl-centric approach but didn't have a chance to formulate an alternate plan before the young Vanuatuans were at our window. They were all grinning, showing off teeth so white that you'd think they brushed with bleach.

"Hello," Jo began, doing her best to match their megawatt smiles.

"Hi," I hastily added, not wanting to appear inarticulate or, God forbid, younger than Jo.

"Hello hi," the kids chorused back to us. "Hello hi. Hello hi."

Then they went quiet as though waiting for us to say something else.

After a moment's pause, I ventured, "Nice to meet you?"

"Nicetomeetyou," they repeated in a happy jumble, then started laughing. Jo and I just grinned back like the slow-witted cousins from out of town.

A little boy in the front near the door said something in Bislama, the local pidgin English dialect. I must have betrayed my lack of understanding because he repeated himself more emphatically. Despite the increased decibel at which he spoke, I still couldn't understand him. Abandoning all attempt at verbal communication, he simply gestured for us to follow him.

"Can we go?" I asked my parents as I unfastened our seatbelt and winched my fanny pack tightly to my waist.

"Where are you going?" my mother wanted to know, but Dad was less concerned.

"Where are they going to go, Alison? It's an island!"

"I'll come with you," Mom insisted as she got out of the car. Dad stayed behind to talk to Nicholas, who had already started chatting animatedly with some of the local men.

We gave our new friends the thumbs-up as we got out. Happy that we were joining them, they formed a rough honor guard around us as we moved toward the center of the village. My mother walked behind us, smiling at our wardens, while keeping a watchful eye on us. As we made our way between the rough huts, my nose perked up. Mingling with the scents of smoke and livestock was an enticing smell that made my stomach growl in unapologetic hunger.

But what if this was the scent of seared missionary? Were these seemingly friendly children just an elaborate ruse to get us into the cauldron?

I was contemplating making a break for the relative safety of the jeep – though Nicholas was probably in on the cannibalistic festivities, too – when we rounded a corner and I realized that the source of these delicious smells was a sturdy cast-iron skillet hanging over an open flame.

For a second I wondered how they fit a missionary into a pot that small, and then I saw a half-naked cook gracefully flip over a misshapen lump.

Could be an ear? Or maybe a big toe? I almost didn't care; it smelled divine.

The chef waited until the deep-fried morsels were golden brown, then deftly pulled them out of the seething oil and piled them on a banana leaf next to her.

"Johnnycake," one of the children explained.

Let's hope that Johnny didn't used to be a missionary, I thought.

When the kids indicated we should take one, I only hesitated for a moment. Sorry, Johnny. Picking up one of the larger treats, I took a big bite. Crispy on the outside with a warm interior like spongy bread, it possessed the smallest hint of sweetness and no discernible taste of an unfortunate missionary. This was simply Pentecost Island's answer to Dunkin' Donuts.

Josephine and the other kids grabbed their own treats, and we all squatted in the dirt to wolf them down. In between scarfing, I managed to exclaim, "Awesome."

"Awe-some," one of the older boys repeated with a perfectly white grin.

As I sat there trying not to stare at the supernatural ivory sheen of their chompers, I realized that I must have looked equally peculiar to these island children. I was decked out in blue athletic Adidas shorts with white stripes down the side, a T-shirt advertising a Pennsylvania youth soccer league, Coke bottle glasses, and a triumphantly neon-blue fanny pack. I'd topped off my ensemble with a baseball cap boasting bright yellow lightning bolts on each side. The hat was intentionally eye-catching so that my mom could find me in a crowd. Ironically, the hat always drew a crowd, so it was a somewhat self-defeating accessory.

Despite the fact that I was a half-wit when it came to fashion, Josephine was practically a runway ingénue. Her soft round face was framed by a tumble of brown curls that seemed to give her a halo. She wore a simple embroidered white linen top that my mother had picked up on one of our trips and a cerulean skirt that set off the white perfectly. Jo just had a natural grace and poise that I could never muster. I was Luke Skywalker when he was still working on Uncle Owen's moisture farm, and she was Princess Leia. We were an oddly contrasting duo, made all the more strange by our proximity to the island's native children, who had a refreshing ignorance about the concept of modern style.

When we were done with our johnnycakes, we wiped our greasy hands on our legs and stood up. Remembering the ritual from the Air Fiji flight, I made sure to bow deeply to the chef, who seemed pleased, if not a little confused, by my gesture. Bowing to our small horde of hosts, I discovered they knew the ritual because they all bowed right back.

Not wanting to be rude, I bowed again. They bowed in turn. I bowed once more. They responded. I was beginning to wonder if this ceremony was endless when my mother jumped in.

"That's enough, Nevin," she said with a light pat on the shoulder, like the ones coaches give kids when they strike out playing Wiffle ball. "I'm sure they get the point."

"That you're an idiot," my sister added. "This isn't Japan."

"Bite me."

Mom put the kibosh on a larger argument. "Nevin. Josephine. Stop it."

She herded my sister, me, and our gaggle of new friends back to the jeep, where my father creatively conversed with a few of the local men about fishing. From what I could see, the conversation consisted of single words, smiles, and emphatic hand gestures.

"Big?" Dad asked, holding his arms a few feet apart to indicate the size of the fish he was imagining.

"Big big," one of the men replied with a chuckle, waving his arms open wide toward the heavens, perhaps implying that the fish he caught was larger than an out-of-towner could conceive.

"Ahhh," my father replied with no small amount of wonder, probably fantasizing over catching a sky-sized skipjack.

My sister and I piled back into the jeep and waved goodbye to the johnnycake posse from our front-seat perch.

"You know, you are the first white children to ever come here," Nicholas told us as we headed over to the dive site. "They have never seen anyone like you."

Same here, I thought. Though I'd met kids of every hue – and been on the It's A Small World ride at the Magic Kingdom several times – I'd never been in the middle of a johnnycake-eating throng of youngsters like this one. Today had been a once-in-a-lifetime experience for all of us.

The *naghol* was to be held at Wali, a region a few miles south of the village. It took another half an hour of bouncing around in the jeep before Nicholas suddenly pulled over to the side of the road. "We'll walk the rest of the way," he told us as he got out.

We followed him, our shoes sinking half a foot into the mire. With every step, there was a sloppy sucking noise followed by a small pop. If I weren't so worried about falling into the gunk, I probably would have been making fart jokes.

Our guide led us along a slender, sludgy trail that led into the jungle. It angled up a hill steeply, but it was impossible to see where we were going because the vegetation was so thick. Peeking above us, it was hard to even see the sky except for the occasional blue blip. This was definitely not somewhere I wanted to get lost – or spend the night.

Then suddenly a clearing opened before us and a 100-foot-tall tower loomed into view. It looked equally impressive and unstable. It was built on the side of a hill with the diving side facing the downward slope, and a freshly cut tree ran down its core, forming the backbone of the spindly structure. Constructed of small, freshly cut saplings, it was held together by jungle creepers, or *lianas* as the islanders called them. Not a single nail was used.

Though many visitors would be hard-pressed to believe that land diving is a precision sport given the primitive building materials, they would be mistaken. According to what Kirk Huffman had told us the day before, building the tower was a time-honored science honed by fervent belief and the necessity of invention. The construction process took more than a month, with most of the tribe's men chipping in.

The vines were a vital part of the jump, so they had to be selected with care. A creeper that is a tad too long or brittle – instead of well cut and supple – could result in a spinal injury or worse for an unfortunate jumper. This was especially true since these aerialists plummeted without the luxury of a helmet or a net to soften the impact should something go awry.

The ideal jump ends with the diver's arms crossed and head bowed to the chest, so just the tips of his shoulders grazed the ground below him. In this way, he blesses the ground, ensuring an abundance of yams for his community. The higher the dive, the more plentiful the harvest. In case this blessing ended as a cursed jump, the ground below the tower was meticulously churned up to create a softer surface for those who did more than brush shoulders with it.

"Each part of the tower represents a different part of the human body," Nicholas explained, pointing up the structure as we walked toward it. "The feet are the bottom, and the top is the head."

He went on to explain that the tower was divided into a series of rough platforms arrayed from tip to toe. Once he put it into perspective, it did look a bit like Castle Grayskull crossed with Sauron's stronghold in *The Lord of the Rings*. According to our knowledgeable guide, each man built his own jumping platform in this unpromising structure and chose his own vines to ensure that he was the only one to blame in the event of an accident. It's also taboo to touch someone else's jumping materials because demonic contamination might occur, which could lead to a bad jump. And a bad jump could be a final jump.

I made a mental note not to touch anything. While I would have loved to be immortalized in legend, I didn't think that being the white devil who screwed up the yam harvest was the way to go about it.

According to Nicholas, the older men jumped first from the uppermost reaches. The younger divers started out jumping from "only a few stories up," though even that proposition sounded patently insane to me.

How did the tribe handle boys who didn't want to dive? Were they pushed? Were they exiled off the island? Maybe they were fed to the sharks or staked out at the bottom of the tower to be devoured by fire ants?

The dire possibilities were endless, and I couldn't decide which gruesome fate was most likely, so I broached the topic with Nicholas.

"What happens if a boy doesn't want to jump?"

Nicholas grinned like the Cheshire Cat. "Vanuatu boys are very brave. Everyone jumps."

I gulped. "You don't make visitors jump, do you?"

This must have been the funniest thing that Nicholas ever heard because he let out a loud hoot of laughter. He patted me on the shoulders. "Don't worry. You stay on the ground."

He chuckled again and went over to talk to some of the men tilling up the earth. They all started laughing and turned to give me what they must have intended to be reassuring smiles. It was either that or they were beaming because they were thinking of how fun it would be to drag me up the tower and make a man out of me. I skittered away sideways like a spooked crab to the meager protection of my family.

I tried to make myself inconspicuous by burying my head in the guidebook to learn more about what I was witnessing. My sister stayed near me, reading *From the Mixed-Up Files of Mrs. Basil E. Frankweiler*. A short distance away, my mother sat under her own tree, alternately scribbling furiously in her diary and staring balefully at my father, who was photographing the preparations.

The ever-helpful team at Fodor's claimed that there's a tradition that men may say whatever they wish with impunity before they jump. These could be their last words, so it's a chance for them to unburden their souls of any baggage they are carrying around without fear of judgment or reprisal. They could admit to adultery, theft, or even murder, but they'd be forgiven when they dove for the greater good of the tribe.

But what if they made the admission – "It was I who stabbed Frank to death with the spear" – but then didn't jump? What if they were suddenly overcome with the weight of what they'd done, freaked out, and couldn't bring themselves to go through with the dive? Did they still get immunity, or would the rules change without the dive in the equation? Which means that after all that, they could climb down, only to be stabbed to death by Frank's

31

brother, John, who would then climb the tower, admit his wrongdoing, dive, and therefore be forgiven for the murder he had just committed. I wasn't sure, but I didn't want to get close enough to Nicholas to ask him.

After about two hours of preparation, everyone finally stopped working and started crowding around the base of the tower. The men from the village formed two rough lines with the bare-breasted women standing in a row behind them. Each man held a long stick, like a sturdy walking cane, which came up to his chest. They began a rising and falling singsong chant punctuated by syncopated hoots, yelps, and whistles. As they sang, they moved side to side, their feet stamping to the rhythm as they brought their sticks down to the ground to emphasize the beats. All of these men – and the boys who would be men – would be jumping today, but none of them looked nervous. In fact, they looked thrilled to be there.

Suddenly, my own rituals of manhood seemed so small and insignificant in comparison: riding a bike without the training wheels, being allowed to light the fuses on fireworks, and shoplifting candy bars from the local newsstand to impress my classmates. Sure, I might break my leg if I fell off my black BMX. I could "blow my only hands off," as my mother put it. And I guess there was a chance for some time in a juvenile detention facility if I got busted with a pocketful of stolen candy bars. But these were all wildly improbable events, and they were the most extreme negative outcomes possible. When you're land diving, serious injury – and even death – are very real possibilities.

What death-defying act would I be willing to do in order to ensure that my town would have its own version of a bountiful yam harvest? Maybe dive off the high board at the swimming pool? I would definitely not take a gainer off a tower in the middle of the jungle with only vines strapped to my ankles. These divers were exhibiting a real selflessness through their jumps, and I couldn't find a parallel for in my own life's experiences. I couldn't imagine risking life and limb for the sake of my fellow man.

My sister scooted closer, ending my reverie. "Pretty crazy that those guys are gonna jump, huh?"

"Yeah. I've never been happier to be a tourist."

"You couldn't pay me enough." She shook her head. "It looks so crazy, I wouldn't even want you to do it."

We turned to watch the dancers, whose pace had started to pick up. One of them broke free of the line and walked over to the base of the tower. He was an older man and his short hair was streaked with gray, but he looked fit enough to run back-to-back marathons before breakfast. He grabbed the wooden struts and began to pull himself up the side of the structure, using his feet to find niches where the sticks were lashed together with vines. As he climbed, he called out in short bursts and the dancers below replied with cries of their own.

With wide eyes, I followed his progress up the sinister tower. It was spindly and sharp, with no soft edges to reassure either the divers or the audience below. When the man reached a platform in the uppermost reaches – somewhere between where I imagined the tower's eye sockets – he disappeared for a few minutes into the interior of the structure to retrieve his vines.

I envisioned him perched up there all alone with nothing but the sun and the wind to give him comfort. He would be tying the vines to his ankles, probably wondering if he'd cut them the right length. Too long and he would be greeted with a rough ending. If he didn't cut them long enough, his body wouldn't touch the ground, so the harvest wouldn't be as blessed. Both options were unattractive, but at this point, there was nothing he could do.

The diver emerged from the depths of the tower with a whoop. He walked to the edge of the platform, a small black outline against the bright blue sky. I could hear my sister suck in her breath and hold it; I was doing the same. The dancers' singing grew louder and more animated, perhaps offering encouragement to the diver or alerting their gods that now was the moment to pay attention.

The man stood poised with his back straight a moment longer before gently leaning forward. He fell with his body curved inward, a half-fetal position. For a moment, he was midway between the sky and the earth, and then the vines straightened out, jerking him to an abrupt halt. His head and shoulders barely skimmed the softened soil before he was yanked upward in a jarring rebound. Only a few feet above the ground he seemed to hold his position, twisting slightly before tumbling back down again. My sister and I both released our captive breaths with loud whooshes as the crowd cheered.

The vines went taut, and two dancers helped the diver stand as he yelled ecstatically. They disentangled his legs from the creepers, and when he was free, he began dancing in place. Then they all rejoined the other dancers on the hill, seamlessly reintegrating themselves into the rhythm of the dance and the cadence of the chanting.

"Ah-woo-ah-woo," the diver yelled toward the heavens triumphantly as he skipped about. I wanted to add my voice to his, but I didn't know if that would violate the rules and muck up the yam harvest.

"I can't believe he just did that," my sister half-whispered next to me.

"Me neither," I agreed, without turning to look at her, still unable to stop watching this man who had just defied death and now looked like he was raving at the greatest party on earth. "That was frickin' awesome."

Over the next hour, a series of men made their way up the tower only to plunge back to the earth. Some dove silently while others let out bloodcurdling howls on the way down. A few of them miscalculated their vine lengths and hit the ground with damp thuds that made me flinch. A couple of times, one or both vines broke, slamming the divers against the tower or into the dirt. But no matter what, they got up immediately, often springing up from their points of impact like crazed jack-in-the-boxes.

After all the men had jumped, it was time for the boys. I had been excited to see the older tribesman prove that they had the biggest balls in the Pacific, but seeing someone my own age jump was beyond the pale. An already impressive feat of bravery just got a million times more inspiring. The first boy to go looked like he was even younger than me, maybe only eight or nine years old. He wasn't dressed like the youngsters back at the village. Like the men, he was wearing nothing more than a bark penis sheath.

I was beyond impressed. "Dude, that's…"

"Insane," Jo finished, sounding awed.

The boy scuttled nimbly up the tower like a monkey. He seemed so eager and excited, and his quick, agile movements belied no fear. I was impressed with even this element of his achievement, which would have earned him a Presidential Fitness Award back in the States. By comparison, I had a hard time doing pull-ups and could never shimmy up the rope in gym class.

When the young diver reached a platform about three stories up from the ground, he sat down and started tying vines around his ankles. Even from where I was standing, I could see that his movements were graceful and confident. Finished with his meager preparations, the diver stood up and pulled out a dark feather he had wedged behind his ear. He leaned forward and dropped it off the edge to see which way the winds were blowing.

We all watched it tumble downward, swishing this way and that as it was lightly buffeted by the sea breeze that swept in from the coast. It touched down about 10 feet away from the base of the tower and a little to the jumper's left. He looked down at it, seemed satisfied with the result, and stepped to the edge of the platform.

I looked over at Josephine; her eyes were locked on the boy. Both our mouths were hanging open, slack-jawed in a mix of awe and anxiety. The natives below raised the volume of their chanting, and the beat of their feet moved faster and faster. This was the diver's moment of truth, his chance to prove that he was no longer a boy.

He clapped his hands once, gave a shrill hoot, and then fell forward, his arms almost lazily crossing his chest as he rocketed downward. The vines straightened out, there was a snapping noise, and then the boy's head swung only a few inches from the ground.

This time I couldn't help but cheer, my voice mixing in with those of the dancers at the base of the tower. Who cares if I was violating protocol? When you blow up the Death Star, a good yell is in order. The young diver was helped up, and he started dancing, taking his rightful place with the tribe's men. He had passed the test and cleared the hurdle from youth to manhood. Next time he would have to jump from much higher up – some reward.

"Ah-woo-ah-woo-ah-way," the successful jumper yelled.

"Ah-woo-ah-woo-ah-way," the Vanuatuans called back, the men triumphantly pointing their sticks toward the sky as if challenging the thundercloud passing over the sun at that moment. Apparently, the weather gods didn't take too kindly to this affront because the heavens opened up, drowning the proceedings in a sudden deluge of tropical rain.

It happened so quickly that it was like two separate film sequences had been spliced together. On the upside, I could only assume that yams required a healthy amount of water to flourish, so the tribe's prayers were being answered. Mission accomplished, land divers!

Because we were underneath the protective cover of the jungle canopy, my sister and I were spared the worst of the downpour. My mother had her own natural foliage umbrella and was equally unworried by the storm. Dad wasn't as lucky. He swore loudly as he tucked his camera under his shirt and made a beeline for the protection of an overhanging frond.

Turning back to watch the land-diving ritual, we suddenly realized that Dad getting his photography gear waterlogged was the least of anyone's worries.

The abrupt squall was accompanied by a strong wind that whipped the trees around us with a furious energy and battered the tower ruthlessly. The structure swayed in this sudden maelstrom, creaking back and forth like a broken metronome. The islanders below were unconcerned by the rain, but they had stopped dancing and seemed to be powwowing about their dive site, which suddenly looked like it was one broken vine away from a Jenga.

"Do you think it's going to crash on them?" I asked Jo in a hushed tone, somehow thinking that talking loudly might be the final straw that sent it tumbling over.

She gave me a worried look, her brow furrowed in consternation. "I hope it doesn't fall on any animals in the jungle."

Only Jo would worry about a stray parrot before a fellow human. "Way to prioritize, dude."

We returned our attention to the tower's drunken dance on the hillside because it looked like some agreement had been reached. There were a lot of solemn nodding and stick pounding going on. The group broke apart, discarded their canes, and shooed the women back.

The men gathered at the base of the tower like a pack of foot soldiers getting ready to storm the castle gates. I could hear them yell over the torrent, nothing discernible, probably their equivalent of "Heave ho." The whole mass of men then pushed against the wobbly structure.

For a moment nothing happened, then the tower started to tip toward the slope. The men moved back as the tower fell forward. It swept downward with the same slow-motion grace as one of the divers, a wooden sword cutting through the rain. With a wet, cracking crash, it struck the ground, spraying up bits of mud and cracked branches. It seemed to be straining to bounce back up, but it settled down.

Although this unexpected destruction of the tower clearly signaled the end of their annual ritual, the Vanuatuans cheered wildly. Oddly enough, the rain stopped and the clouds moved away from the sun at the same time; the storm was over as quickly as it had started. Suddenly it was hot, damp, and bright. My mother came over to us as my father emerged from the jungle with his camera, which had survived its dousing. We all reunited with a mix of awe and amazement etched on our faces.

"That was something, wasn't it?" Dad asked no one in particular. "I think I got some great shots."

Mom was clearly more worried about us than the spectacle. "Are you okay?"

I gave her a sticky hug. "We're fine. At least I didn't have to jump."

She pulled my father and sister in for a four-way hug. "That was really special. Just wait till you tell your classmates about this."

"Yeah, this will definitely get me an A+ for show and tell if I can take in some of Dad's pictures," Jo burbled excitedly. "Can I? Can I?"

"Of course," Dad said, clearly flattered by the request. "I'll have them blown up and matted for you."

He was still glowing with fatherly pride when Nicholas joined us, bearing urgent news. "There's another storm coming. If you want to get off the island today, we have to leave now."

My father looked crestfallen at this turn of events, but I didn't understand why. We'd seen the land diving and the toppling of the tower. By my count, I had made out like a bandit if you included the johnnycakes and the fact that I didn't have to hurl myself into the void.

We said our thank yous and farewells and then practically sprinted down the trail – sploshing, splashing, and praying we didn't take a spill every step of the way. By the time we got to the jeep, we were soggy and dirty from top to bottom but totally exhilarated.

Nicholas peeled out like he was racing in the Indy 500. The road was even more treacherous than it had been that morning, the rain having added a slip 'n' slide factor. The jeep fishtailed this way and that as we jounced around inside. Our guide was hell-bent for leather, and if the options were a dirt floor on Pentecost or a comfy bed back on Efate, I was all for the liberal use of the accelerator.

When we pulled up to the field, the pilot had just landed. He drove the plane right up to us and didn't bother getting out or turning off the engine. We bid Nicholas farewell and thanked him.

My mother and sister gave him hugs, while my father gave him a manly handshake-half-hug combo. When Nicholas came to me, he shook my hand gravely, but there was a glint in his eye. "If you ever want to jump, you can always come back."

Yeah, right! I thought even as I replied, "Thanks for the generous offer. I'll be in touch!"

We boarded the Duct Tape Express, and I ended up in the co-pilot's seat. I pulled on my seatbelt and waved to Nicholas from my window.

The plane moved through the muck to the far side of the clearing, where an old striped athletic sock fluttering from a bamboo stake acted as the windsock. The pilot turned toward the forest at the end and gunned the engine. The Cessna picked up speed, jolting across the uneven terrain as we rushed toward the tree line. We were going faster and faster and the trees were coming at us like they were going to be the last scene in the movie of my life, but suddenly our ride got smooth as I felt the wheels lift off, and the plane shot over the tops of the palms and into the wide blue beyond.

The pilot turned to me after we'd climbed up several thousand feet, his lips curling into a conspiratorial smile beneath his mirrored aviator glasses.

"Do you want to try this?" he yelled, nodding with his head toward the yoke. There was an identical one in front of me, but I had carefully avoided touching it with the same discretion I had shown for vines and towers on Pentecost. I turned around to seek approval from my parents, but they were busy staring out the windows.

How many kids could say that they'd flown a plane? I wondered.

Not many, a little voice whispered. *Only men fly planes.*

This was it; this was my test! I glanced down at the ocean below us. Copper blue hues and flecks of white-tipped waves danced across its surface. It seemed like such a long way to fall.

Be a man for your tribe, my danger-loving Jiminy Cricket urged. *Do it!*

This was my chance. I couldn't say no. Like that boy on the tower, I had to take a leap of faith.

Uttering a quick prayer to the generic god who oversaw the day-to-day needs of agnostics, I took a deep breath and firmly grabbed the yoke with both hands. The vibrations of the plane pulsed through my arms. I could feel it twitching like it wanted to take control of its own destiny. But it was in my hands now; I was in command.

I looked over at the pilot, who still had one hand on the wheel. He gave me an okay sign with his other hand.

"Way to go, captain," he yelled. "You're doing great."

I smiled. I may have arrived on Pentecost a boy, but now I was a man.

I turned back to the skyway in front of me, where the blood orange sun was just starting its slow descent toward the horizon.

Even though I wasn't wearing a bark penis sheath, I whooped triumphantly, "Ah-woo-ah-woo-ah-way," but no one could hear me over the roar of the engines.

Pass the Kava on the Left-Hand Side

[Fiji 1986, Age 12]

Since retiring and moving the family to New Zealand a year earlier, my father had been dividing his days into two activities: fishing and everything else. It didn't matter if he was casting from the shore into a small pond, taking out a motorboat to go trolling on a lake, or wading into a river to go fly fishing. No matter where we were in the world, if there was a body of water offering even the slightest possibility of a bite, he had to fish in it.

Regardless of how many of these aquatic adventures ended in abject failure, he remained eternally optimistic.

"It looks promising," he'd declare when he discovered a new potential spot. "I'm not sure if anyone's ever even fished here before."

There's a reason for that, I'd think to myself, while saying aloud, "You could be the first, Dad."

That's how we had ended up on Matangi island, a horseshoe-shaped microdot perched in the northeastern reaches of the sprawling Fijian archipelago, accessible only by a 20-minute boat ride from Taveuni island, a destination that was already pretty far off the beaten path. I was worried that being in the middle of nowhere meant that we would be denied some of the most basic creature comforts, like electricity. I raised this worry with the owner, Noel, when we arrived.

"Don't worry," he tried assuring me. "We actually do have a generator here, but it's very unreliable. During the last hurricane, we lost power for several weeks until they could bring over some parts that we had to order from Brisbane."

This didn't alleviate my concerns.

Noel ushered us over to our accommodations as I wondered where I could find a candle to allow me to read at night. As soon as I saw our lodgings though, I knew that an open flame would be out of the question. With woven walls, thatched roofs, and open doorways, the *bures* looked like tropical tinderboxes. I didn't doubt that one misplaced spark would turn one of them into a smoking pile of ashes. The interiors were simple – just mosquito netting-covered beds with small tables next to each one – but clean and airy. There wasn't a fire extinguisher to be seen.

Standing in the doorway, my father surveyed the surrounding scenery.

"This is something else, isn't it?" he remarked.

Pointing to the glimmering surface of the South Pacific, which was visible through a break in the palm trees, he exclaimed, "Gosh, the sea is right there. Amazing. It looks promising."

A dream of a deep-sea fishing expedition was the reason he had directed our trip to this remote isle off a remote island in a far-flung Melanesian kingdom. Noel was more than happy to stoke his enthusiasm.

"These waters are untouched," he told my father, who grinned back at him with the eagerness of a child contemplating gobbling up an entire banana split alone. "You'll get whatever you want." He ticked off the list on his hand. "Barracuda. Skipjack tuna. Dolphinfish. Blue marlins are a possibility. So are wahoo."

Dad didn't miss a beat. "Sign us up."

Wait, *us?* Why was I getting dragged into this?

"It'll be fun for the kids," he continued, giving my heart some small satisfaction even as it sank into the depths of my chest cavity. At least Jo would have to suffer through this hell with me.

* * * * *

The sun had barely begun its arc up from the horizon when Dad gently shook me awake the next morning.

"Time to get up," he urged in the dim light that suffused our hut. "Those fish aren't going to catch themselves."

One could only wish, I thought as I began getting ready.

He moved over to Josephine's cot and repeated his rousing routine. I could hear her grumbling as he pulled back the covers.

"Breakfast is in 10 minutes, so get dressed," Dad instructed before heading out the door. "Don't make me come back in here."

Climbing out of bed, I chose a pair of dandelion yellow swim trunks and a white T-shirt emblazoned with two hibiscuses. Josephine continued the floral theme by donning a flowing pink dress edged with an embroidered flower pattern. We wordlessly slathered ourselves with suntan lotion, knowing that Mom would give us a full inspection before sending us off for our re-creation of *The Old Man and the Sea*.

Sure enough, that was her first concern when we walked over to the wall-less kitchen that was abuzz with activity. "Did you get it on your neck and on the tips of your ears? What about behind your legs? Are your arms covered completely?"

We nodded compliantly, twirling in place to show that we had the appropriate sunscreen sheen.

"Okay," she conceded before turning back to Dad. "What I wouldn't do for an espresso right now."

"You're right about that," he agreed, despondently looking down at his mug brimming with steaming brown sludge. "I could use a double."

It wasn't all bad news. The cooking fire was billowing smoke, carrying with it the promise of sausage and eggs. Soon we were tucking into plates of links and sunny side ups, filled out with fresh-baked rolls, guava slices, and canoes of papaya glossy from a spritz of freshly squeezed lime. Josephine and I drank passion fruit juice from tiny glass cups, which looked as if they'd been designed for pygmies. I hadn't even finished the few sips the glass contained, much less my breakfast, when Noel appeared to whisk us off.

"Hope you're ready," he announced. Dressed in a pair of well-worn khakis with a patched left knee and a white *guayabera* shirt that had seen better days, he looked like a late-in-life Hemingway. His appearance further fired up my father's indefatigable zeal.

"I can remember pulling marlins out of the Florida Keys that were longer than a car," he reminisced. "God, that was something. We'd cut them up right there on the docks and have them for dinner."

His trawl down memory lane continued as we made our way to the dock. Josephine and I distanced ourselves from his now-familiar tall tales by strolling far behind with Mom. It was light out now, the sun's orange tropical glow adding a warm hue to everything it touched. The grass was as short as well-worn AstroTurf, but softer. A strong breeze blew in from the sea, swaying the tops of the palm trees above us.

It was the most tranquil of scenes – until a coconut rocketed by me, just grazing my right shoulder. I half-leaped, half-twitched to my left and let out an embarrassingly high-pitched yelp in midair.

"Holyhellwhatwasthat?!!?"

Striking the ground with a dull thud, the life-threatening projectile bounced once, rolled a short distance away, and lay still. I backed away from it, as if it might suddenly sprout wings and rocket toward me again.

"It's okay," my mother reassured me.

Jo snorted loudly. "You're such a wimp."

That's when another tropical missile hit the earth right next to her. She shot straight up, like Wile E. Coyote being blown into the heavens by his own dynamite.

"That's called karma," I taunted.

My mother wasn't interested in our bickering. "Move it!"

We started hustling toward the break in the trees that opened up onto the beach. I could hear the rustle of leaves and the slap of the fronds against the trunks above us. A few more coconuts came loose, hitting the ground near us. I imagined there were large clusters of them hanging up there like warheads. None of us wanted to end up as a page 11 *National Enquirer* article (Cuckoo Nuts! Tourists Brained to Death!), so we frantically ratcheted up our pace every time another bomb sailed down from above.

Bursting out from the trees and away from the artillery assault, we were nonchalantly greeted by Dad.

"Training for the Olympics?" he asked.

"No, Ralph, there was a hailstorm of coconuts," my mother shot back.

"They're always falling," Noel chipped in, as if he were telling us that the sky was usually blue in this part of the world.

He tapped his head. "My cousin was hit once. Never was the brightest guy. Now he takes care of the chickens; that's about all he's good for."

Jo and I must have looked petrified because he gave us a smile. "Enough about that. Let's go fishing."

The boat was moored at the end of a worn wooden pier jutting out into the turquoise of the South Pacific. A small cabin stood in the front, and a covered deck with open sides at the back housed the elevated captain's chair, where we would do battle with the fish. The seat was covered in faded white pleather, cracked from constant exposure to the sea air and salt water.

A couple of Noel's helpers were loading equipment on board. I wondered if either of them was the coconut victim. Both men had closely cropped hair that didn't seem to be hiding any blunt force trauma scars, but maybe they had healed in the intervening years.

While Dad continued to chat up Noel on the dock about his Floridian adventures, Josephine and I clambered on board. We proceeded to thoroughly explore what little there was to see of the cabin, where I imagined we'd have to huddle if an unexpected tropical storm ran into us.

The front of the small space was filled by the steering wheel, the CB radio hanging from the ceiling above it, and a well-worn radar screen on the window ledge. The floor was covered in carpet so splatter stained that it was hard to discern the original pattern. Small padded benches ran down either side. The scent of fish and diesel mixed, lingering like a pervasive, pungent perfume.

"I feel like a sardine in here," Jo announced before popping back outside. Following her, I gulped fresh air and watched seagulls skimming the waves while the rest of the day's supplies were stowed onboard.

"Promise me that you'll be careful," Mom urged us from the dock. "Do exactly what Noel tells you."

I gave a thumbs-up. "No prob, Mom."

"Stop worrying, Alison," my father interjected. "I'll be with them the whole time."

"That's what concerns me." She drew a purple hankie out of the recesses of her beach bag and gave a quick goodbye flutter. "I'm kidding. Have fun. I'll see you when you get back."

The boat pulled away from the dock a short while later, the rumble of diesel engines accompanied by the cries of the gulls and the frothy churning of the wake.

As we headed out toward the sun where it shimmered on the horizon and away from the small protections of the island, it did feel like a grand adventure was in the offing. I was Captain Ahab in search of Moby Dick! Then I remembered what happened to the peg-legged maniac and the *Pequod*. Maybe I'd be Ishmael instead, though that literary parallel didn't bode well for my companions.

My father, Josephine, and I stood in the shade on the rear casting deck, Dad in the center with his arms draped across our shoulders. We stared into the blue water racing by, wondering what it might have in store for us. The tiny triangular tips flashed like diamonds in the sunlight, equally mesmerizing and discombobulating in this fast-forward state. After a few minutes gazing into its depths, I had to disengage in hopes of quelling a growing headache.

Padding along the wooden deck stained with the guts and gore of countless fishing expeditions, I found a shady corner on the foredeck. I leaned against the cabin, which seemed to be cleanest surface on the entire vessel.

I soon figured out why. As the boat hit a dip, a wash of spray came over the bow and doused me from head to toe.

"You don't want to stand there," Noel unhelpfully told me a second later when he walked by. "You'll get soaked."

He paused and looked me up and down. "You probably figured that out already."

No shit, Sherlock. I nodded as I attempted to wipe off my glasses with my wet T-shirt. So much for my quiet moment.

"Don't worry. This sea air will dry you off quickly." He turned to walk away. "Ready to do some fishing?"

"I guess so. That's why we're here, right?"

At the back of the boat, I found my father conferring with one of Noel's helpers. Dad was holding an ivory-toned fishing rod, which was almost twice as long as I was tall. The two of them were choosing which lures we would use from a weather-beaten tackle box on the deck. The case was full of colorful choices, flecked with neon racing stripes, blinged out with patches of liquid silver, and sporting Seuss-ian tails.

After much debate, Dad decided to first try one with a gleaming, googly-eyed metallic head and a streaming tail that made it look like a futuristic squid.

"This should do the trick," he said as he attached it to the end of the line. "What fish could resist this?"

Casting off the stern, he sent the lure arcing over the bubbled froth of our wake. It landed with a small splash, immediately sinking below the surface.

"We'll have dinner in no time," he told me and Jo, who had materialized at my side.

Keeping the rod at a 45-degree angle, he intently peered down the end of his line, waiting for any signs of movement that would indicate he might have dinner. With the deck gently swaying, he stood there with his legs braced and slightly spread apart. His shoulders were relaxed, but having watched him fish before, I knew that he could go from chill to adrenalized in a heartbeat.

Josephine had a look of concern on her face as she watched. "Are we going to eat the fish?"

My father didn't turn to answer her. "Of course."

"Duh," I added.

That elicited a swift series of punches that weren't so much painful as they were annoying. "Bastard."

"Josephine, stop hitting your brother," Dad half-heartedly ordered, his eyes still locked on the line. "And no swearing."

Putting my hands up to create punching mitts to deflect her crabapple-sized fists, I smiled. "Yeah, Jo, you heard him."

"Whatever. I'm going to push you off the boat."

"I'd like to see you try."

Before we could engage in a test of strength and will, my father's line snapped taut as his rod bent downward toward the wave tops.

"Got something!"

Flexing his sun-weathered hands around the cork-covered handle, he leaned back in almost theatrical slow motion. The muscles along his arm tightened, his shoulders tensed, and his knuckles whitened. He pulled the rod toward his chest, the line slackened briefly, and he reeled in furiously. The fish changed its tack, crossing our wake until it was off our starboard side.

Dad yanked up again. "Sonofabitch."

"No swearing," Jo muttered under her breath, only loud enough that I could hear it.

"Cut the engines," Noel commanded, moving his hand across his throat as he turned toward the cabin.

The rumble decreased to a purr and then silence as the boat slowed to a halt. The line crisscrossed through the air as the fish rocketed to the port side, then moved away. There was an aggravated squeal as the line slowly spooled out. Dad didn't lose his grip though. If anything, it intensified. He heaved up again, created a momentary dip, and cranked the handle.

A zigzag pattern emerged as he worked his catch slowly closer to our vessel. Ten, then 15 minutes passed as he battled with his subaquatic nemesis. It looked like excruciating work, but he still managed to turn to us in the middle of his South Pacific skirmish.

"Pretty amazing, isn't it? There are not a lot of kids who can say they've done this!"

"Definitely not, Dad," I agreed, doing my best to disguise my sarcasm.

If only he would hurry up and get that fish on board. The slow heave of the boat coupled with the mid-morning sun angling into the covered back deck and the lingering smell of the diesel were taking a toll. The headache had worked its way up through the back of my neck and was nesting at the center of my cranium. Even worse was what was going on in my stomach. It felt like whatever mayhem was brewing was going to end in a nuclear war involving explosions at both ends.

I tried to ignore what was happening inside by concentrating on the action in front of me. As the fish's Z pattern became tighter and tighter, my father became more and more focused. Now the fish was starting to break through the water. It emerged from the depths like a spastic prism, a thousand colors glinting off its shimmering skin as it thrashed violently.

"Mahi-mahi," said Noel. "Nice size."

"It's beautiful," Jo said.

For once, I didn't disagree with her on the principle that it's best to annoyingly contradict your younger sibling whenever you can. The fish was iridescent, almost like an abalone shell. Flecks of dark blue dotted its silver body, which sported a shocking neon green stripe at the bottom. A fanned fin at the top tapered as it ran down its back, ending in a forked tail fin that helped propel it up to nearly 60 miles an hour – when it wasn't hooked on the end of my father's line, of course.

Every time it rose up from the water, it was closer to the side of the boat. Noel had clearly seen this story run its course more than a few times. His actions were quick but measured. He grabbed a gaff and positioned himself just to the right of my father. Brandishing the hooked stick, he looked like a tattoo-less Queequeg rearing back to harpoon Moby Dick.

"Get him in close and I'll grab him."

"Come on, Dad!" I urged.

It was exciting to watch him. Every part of his being was concentrated on that fish. Nothing else mattered. He was in the primal zone. It was man versus beast. His inner caveman had taken over. This wouldn't end until the fish was on the boat or he was pulled into the South Pacific Ocean.

Dad gave a herculean tug on the pole. The mahi-mahi rose out of the water, a shower of glittering drops spraying in every direction as it flipped and flopped in a last-ditch effort to dislodge the hook. For a moment, it hung in the air, tracing a hole in the sky.

Then Noel buried the gaff in its gills. The fish lurched, its arc broken. With a few almost too-quick-to-see movements of the barbed hook, Noel had the fish over the side. It landed on the deck with a wet thwack then somersaulted violently. It hit the wood again with a sharp slap next to me, and I jumped straight up.

While I was still in midair, Noel calmly grabbed a baseball bat and hit the fish three times in the head. The mahi-mahi half curled up for the last time, then sank to the deck.

Almost as soon as the life left its body, the color began draining from its scales. The shiny sparkle was replaced by a bright jungle green that soon faded into a darker shade of pond algae. No longer did it look majestic; now it looked gross and slimy. The odor that began to emanate from it was equally unappetizing, a fermented briny stench that did not pair well with the rise and fall of the ship.

Proffering my father an undersized beer bottle, Noel seemed oblivious to all of this. "Want a stubby?"

My father accepted it, taking a long sip while he surveyed his catch.

"It's beautiful, isn't it?"

Jo and I exchanged a glance that seemed to say, "Yes, Dad. But only if you believe a quick brutal death is more beautiful than life."

He missed our silent communication.

"Who's up next? Nevin?"

"Do I have to?"

A look of irritation crossed his face. "If you didn't want to fish, why did you come along?"

Like we had a choice, I thought as I said, "I'm not feeling great. Can Jo go first?"

"Fine. Jo, you're up." He turned away to discuss his triumph with Noel.

Another well-aimed punch landed just below my shoulder. "Gee, thanks."

I barely noticed. My chief concern at that moment was getting as far away from everyone as was possible on this tiny teacup. I could feel my stomach tossing and turning violently, the fat of the sausages mixing unpleasantly with the acid of the lime, the slimy slither of the scrambled eggs, and the slippery papaya lumps. The contents began to carbonate, bubbling upward.

Scrabbling to the front edge of the boat, I made it just in time to release the jumbled remains of my breakfast into the ocean. Looking down, I watched the chunky orange-brown cloud sully the waters, slowly dissipate, and then disappear like a mist being blown away by a breeze.

I kept my head hanging over the side while I coughed up the final bilious bits. Last to go were two misshapen lumps of papaya, clinging to each other by a string of goo like Siamese twins. To this day, I taste vomit when I eat papaya.

Making my way into the cabin, I plunked myself down on the padded bench and slowly keeled over until I was lying on my back. I closed my eyes, but flashing dots and dashes still floated before me in the darkness. They gently rolled back and forth with the pitch of the boat, doing nothing to quell the nausea that lingered. Though I had nothing left to give the ocean, its motion was still exacting a toll.

I tried to lose myself in the sounds around me – the gentle slap of the waves on the hull, the plaintive cries of the seagulls that kept hovering in hopes of scoring scraps, and the squeaky creak of the wooden deck. Occasionally, I'd hear muffled voices, no doubt my father lecturing Josephine on her fishing form. The steady soundscape was quite hypnotic, so it wasn't long before I had stopped staring at the back of my eyelids and had slipped into sleep.

* * * * *

I'm not sure how long I slept, but it was long enough for my body to find equilibrium. When I awoke, my headache had vanished and the bile in my stomach had subsided. There was still an unpleasant taste that scorched every inch of my palate, so I roused myself in search of something to wash away the vomitus aftermath.

"Hey, sleepyhead," my father quipped when I reappeared. "Feeling better?"

"I think so. Is there anything to drink?"

"Have a Coke," said Noel, our captain-turned-bartender, popping the cap and handing me a curvy glass bottle covered in condensation.

I'm not sure I've ever tasted anything as good as that first sweet sip. I held it in my mouth for a minute, letting the bubbles scour every surface and then swallowed. I could feel my stomach letting out a sigh of relief.

My father gave me a smile. "Better now?"

"Definitely."

"It's your turn. Jo's way ahead of you; she caught a barracuda."

There's no greater inspiration for me than the possibility of being shown up by my younger sister.

"Whatever. I'm going to catch something that'll make the Loch Ness Monster look like a goldfish."

Dad smiled at my bravado, perhaps because it sounded like something he would say. "We'll see. Get in the chair."

Ascending the white fisherman's throne, I situated myself as best I could in a seat designed for someone four times my size. There was a bracket between my legs for the fishing pole and cup holders in either armrest.

To get me started, my father cast the line and then slipped the pole's handle into the holder.

"You can hold onto it, but don't reel in until you see the line move, okay?"

I nodded as I did my best to imitate his grasp on the cork-wrapped handle. My fingers fit all the way around it but just barely. Tracing the line's descent into the waters beyond the boil of the wake, I imagined the prehistoric giants that were swimming beyond my vision. These monsters had flaring neon eyes and teeth as long and sharp as broadswords, and they could move faster than the Millennium Falcon at lightspeed.

Just one would be enough to feed the whole island of Matangi for a month. To thank me for this bounty, I would be crowned king of the ensuing feast. The locals would build a throne on a dais, which would pointedly include a smaller seat at a lower level for my sister. The choicest cuts would be presented to me, and I'd indicate how they would be distributed. Perhaps Josephine would get an eyeball and a part of the brain, if she were lucky.

There was a sharp tug on my line. A beast was mine!

"There's something on there," I squawked excitedly.

Dad put down his beer and came to stand next to me. "Keep your cool. You don't want to lose him."

"You're totally gonna lose him," Josephine scoffed from behind him.

Ignoring her jibe – and hoping to the gods above that I didn't lose the fish so she could hold it over my head forever – I began to slowly reel in. It was difficult work. Whatever was on the other end clearly didn't want to become our dinner. Every turn of the handle was a strain. After every rotation, I paused for a second to shake out my hand so it didn't cramp and give my practically nonexistent muscles a break.

"Do you want help?" Dad offered.

"Nope. I got this."

Slowly, but surely, the line wrapped back around the reel. Every inch was a miniature triumph. After what seemed like forever – but was probably only 10 minutes – the fish finally came into view, a silver streak flickering just below the surface.

Noel ID-ed it as a skipjack tuna, great for grilling. "Get it just a little closer, and I'll take it from there."

The skipjack didn't want to cooperate. Then again, if Vanuatuan cannibals had tried to get me into a giant cauldron, I wouldn't have been helpful either. My arms were getting tired, but the thought of Josephine nagging me for the rest of the trip made me determined to finish the job. A couple more spins of the handle and my prey was just a couple of yards behind us. Noel swooped down with the gaff, hooked the metallic fish in its gills, and tossed it on the deck. Thwack-thwack-thwack went the bat, and quite suddenly, my battle was over.

Gleaming in the sunlight, the tuna looked to be almost two feet long and just under 10 pounds.

"Nice work," my father said, giving me a proud pat on my back. "I knew you'd get him."

I wasn't so sure about that, but I wasn't going to pass up a compliment. Plus, completing my mission to score my share of dinner had more important ramifications in my mind.

"Can we go back now?"

The look of pride on my father's face faded into one of disappointment.

"Yeah, let's go back," Jo chimed in. We didn't always see eye to eye, but this is one thing we could agree on.

She gave Dad a puppy-dog look she had been honing her entire life. "I'm really, really tired."

My father caved but not without a guilt-inducing kiss-off. "Don't be so quick to rush through life," he scolded. "You've got to enjoy these moments."

Like many of the valuable lessons my father taught me, this one took a long time to sink in.

I realized later in life that fishing really has nothing to do with catching anything. It's about unplugging and reconnecting. The act is an excuse to spend time with those you care about, or sometimes just yourself.

Of course, that's not what I was thinking that day as we shifted with the swells of the South Pacific. I just wanted to sit down on solid dry land, where I wouldn't be overcome with the urge to barf.

The boat turned back toward the shore. I perched myself on the side of the boat and contented myself by watching the ocean zip by. The island came into view a short while later, rising on our starboard side like an emerald emerging from the depths. When we pulled up at the dock, Mom was waiting for us, looking relaxed from her day of solitude.

I couldn't get back onto terra firma quick enough. Mom leaned down to give me a hug. As she pulled me in, I could feel her nose twitch.

"Nevin, you reek of vomit. Are you okay?"

"He's fine, Alison," my father piped up. "He got a little seasick; nothing serious."

She released me and gave me a comforting pat on the head. "At least you came back in one piece."

* * * * *

After a late breakfast the next morning – "No papaya for me, thanks!" – Noel announced that we would be feasting on yesterday's catch.

"They won't be ready until early this evening though," he

explained. "In Fiji, we don't cook in regular ovens. Come here; you'll see."

He led us past the kitchen between palm trees and out to the beach. Thankfully, the coconuts above us decided to stay put. Not far from the water's edge, four stakes held up a rusty aluminum roof covering a bare patch of dirt. The pair of helpers from the boat were just finishing digging a circular pit about five feet wide and a foot deep.

I was slightly confused as to what this shallow grave had to do with dinner. "Who died?"

Noel chuckled. "That's the *lovo*. It's an earth oven."

The men began piling small twigs, bits of bark, and dried leaves at the center of the pit. They crosshatched larger sticks on top of this, as if they were weaving the lattice topping for a pie. Freshly chopped chunks of Tahitian chestnut known as *ivi* went on next. They coronated this flammable base with several dozen round rocks that looked like gray boules of sourdough. After lighting the tinder at the very bottom, one man got down on his knees and blew the small flame until it spread throughout the mound.

"Now we wait until the wood has burned down to the embers and the rocks are white hot," Noel explained. "The food goes on top of them."

"It goes directly on the stones?" Jo asked, clearly a little wary about the idea.

"Don't worry, we're not savages here," said Noel. "We wrap the food first. The cook will show you how it's done."

We traced our steps back to the kitchen, where the cook had our catch, steaks, and whole chickens laid out on the counter next to an array of local vegetables. Long yams had been peeled and cut into pale orange circles, there were rectangular chunks of taro, and halved breadfruits displayed their sunburst centers.

Pulling a coconut frond from a pile on the floor, the cook placed my skipjack on the spine of the frond. Taking leaves from either side in each hand, she began to French braid over the top of it, weaving a cage around it. You could still see slivers of silvery skin peeking through the small gaps between the viridian wrapping, but it was almost completely covered. The fronds at each end were woven into a handle, so the packet could be picked up like a spitted hog.

"Once the rocks are ready, we'll put the wrapped food on top of them and cover it all with layers of banana and coconut leaves," explained Noel. "Then we pile sand on top of that to completely trap the heat. Don't worry; the sand doesn't ever touch your food."

I wasn't really that concerned by the idea of the *lovo*. When Dad grilled out on our porch at home, the hamburgers always arrived at the dinner table with char lines and the whiff of smoke. Those always tasted better than the pan-fried patties we made on the stove during the cold weather months when the Weber was hibernating in the garage. A little grit was a part of the deal.

Since we wouldn't be eating until early evening, we had the day to ourselves. My father immediately began peppering Noel with questions about further fishing – maybe from rowboat, raft, or even an inner tube. I had to pull the ripcord since I had no desire to upchuck again.

"Can we hang out on the island today?" I asked my mother. "I'd like to go shelling."

She got the hint. "Good idea. Ralph, I'm going to take the kids to the beach."

My father barely noticed our departure as we strolled back over to our *bure* to don our beachwear and tolerate the inevitable shellacking of sunscreen. From there we took 10 minutes of winding paths to the windward end of the island, where my mother had been told the most shells washed up.

Her intel was right. As we strolled down the sandy strip, it was impossible to take a step without seeing a worthy find. Brown cones splashed with white cow spots mingled with sea-smoothed cat's eyes, dappled cowries, and spiny murex shells that could pierce your skin if you didn't handle their sharp spikes carefully.

I accumulated an impressive array within a short time, each discovery more splendid than the last. As I wandered close to where the tide was gently lapping at the shoreline, there was a speckled band of treasures washed up from the depths. Every color you could imagine was splashed across the beach, but it was a flash of pure white poking up from the wet sand that caught my eye.

Leaning down, I discovered that it was a rounded top with dimpled ridges running out from a small hole in the center that had been indelicately poked open, like when one punctures the tip of an eggshell to blow out its contents. Carefully digging around its edges, I worked my fingers down and underneath. I pulled my find out gently, not sure of what it might be. Crouching by the water's edge, I washed it off to reveal a delicate dome about the size of an Oreo.

"Nice find, Nenne," my mother noted from over my shoulder, using the nickname my sister had given me when she couldn't yet pronounce Nevin. "That's a sea urchin. They're very fragile, so be careful with it."

Zipping open my fanny pack, I looked for a space where I could safely store my newfound treasure.

My mother handed me a napkin from her beach bag. "Use this," she instructed. "That should protect it."

I carefully wrapped the sea urchin and wedged it between a copy of *Island of the Blue Dolphins* and a small coin purse filled with my spending money. I couldn't have been prouder of my discovery, which rivaled finding a gold doubloon in my mind.

Rejoining my sister, we continued walking down the beach. When we reached the end of the peninsula, we took a break to sit down in the shade of the palm trees. Before getting comfortable, I made sure to look into the upper reaches to see if there were any coconut missiles primed for launching. Luckily, the tops were denuded of any potential head trauma inflictors, so I sat down with my back resting against the ridged trunk.

We idled the afternoon away at our little oasis reading in the shade, taking dips in the ocean, and picking up more shells for our collections. When we got hungry, Mom reached into her purple beach bag and pulled out a few bottles of water, a bunch of sweet stubby bananas, their skins bright yellow with black freckles, and a few rolls that she had split open and smeared with now melted butter and sticky guava jam.

Despite her foresight, we were starving by the time we began trudging back down the beach toward the compound around five o'clock. We made a beeline for the *lovo*, which was now a smoking hillock. One of the men was shoveling off the sand, which he set aside in a neat heap. When most of the covering was removed, he bent down and gingerly lifted up the leaves, ensuring that the sand on top didn't spill as he placed them by the pit.

As the smoke was vented from the underground oven, a whiff of the baked fish and the starchy scent of the cassava tickled my nose. It smelled divine.

"*Sa vakaru na kakana,*" the fire tender announced with a toothy grin before adding in halting English, "Food is ready."

Using sheets of aluminum siding as rough platters, we helped carry the still steaming packets back to the kitchen. There they were carefully unwrapped and the contents transferred to well-used plastic plates. As the all-female cook staff began arranging the food buffet-style on the large table, the men began to drift in. I hadn't heard a dinner bell, so I guessed that word just traveled quickly when it was *magiti* time.

The guys brought with them bottom-shelf booze and frosty cans of Fiji Gold beer, which they swigged from liberally while surveying the dinner. One of them passed my father a weathered Coke bottle full of rum. From the expression he made when he took a hearty guzzle, it must have tasted like diesel.

Nonetheless, he managed a smile and a "thank you" that devolved into a hacking cough as he passed the bottle back. That got everyone laughing. Throughout the dinner, various guests tried to have my father give a repeat performance by tempting him with another shot, but he wisely stuck to beer.

When all of the food was neatly arrayed, one of the women cooks told us, "*Mai kana.*"

"That means 'Come and eat,'" Noel helpfully translated as he angled for a prime piece of the mahi-mahi. Since it was cooked whole, the fish's skin had taken on a grayish pallor and its eyes had turned into unappealing Jell-O orbs, making it look like a zombie from *20,000 Leagues Under the Sea.*

Deftly deploying a knife and fork, Noel cut through the skin, maneuvered between the bones, and lifted out a six-inch portion of the midsection. Plunking it down on a plate, he then added heaps of each vegetable, a scoop of coleslaw runny with mayonnaise, and a pair of still steaming buns. He handed the feast on a plate to my mother. "Enjoy."

Dad, Jo, and I followed his lead, passing down the line until our plates were overfilled. I opted for a piece of my tuna, figuring that since I went through all the trouble of killing the fish I should at least honor his passing by eating it. Heading out to the close-cropped lawn, we sat on the ground and proceeded to scarf down everything. As the rest of the dinner guests came out, they took up positions around us.

"Traditionally, men ate before the women," Noel told us between bites, "but we all eat together here."

"I should hope so," my mother replied, using the polite tone that I had come to recognize as one of disapproval.

One of the cooks, a jovial woman with rolling hips and a gap between her two front teeth, plunked down next to us.

"What do you think?" she asked before taking a monstrous bite of taro.

"It's very good," my mother replied. "You'll have to share the recipe for the fish. What spices do you use?"

The food acted as an equalizer and a social lubricant. Suddenly, we weren't just visitors, we were members of the family. Years later, I read about a poll in which Fijians had been voted the friendliest people in the world (Take that, Canada!). I wasn't surprised. My mother chatted with the cook and her crew, Dad traded fishing stories with the men, and my sister and I made small talk with the teenagers in attendance.

One of them stood out because he had chosen to arrive at our de facto dinner table bare-chested, whereas the other men were wearing hole-spotted T-shirts or threadbare hoodies. To draw further attention, he had glazed himself with a thick layer of coconut oil on every available inch of skin. In the dying sunlight of the early evening, he seemed to have a golden glow.

"I'm Cyril," he announced proudly as he deposited his gleaming form down next to my sister.

The contrast between the two of them was striking. Jo was a slender, slightly sun-kissed brunette. He was a deep walnut brown with dark black hair and a gym ad-worthy physique. Also, he was at least twice her age. The 10-year chasm between them didn't seem to bring any social mores to mind for him. He was clearly on the prowl "for a ticket off the island," as my sister put it many years later.

We both introduced ourselves, but his focus stayed locked on Josephine. I got the impression that if a giant hole were to suddenly open up underneath me and swallow me, Cyril wouldn't notice.

"So, where do you come from?" he asked her.

At the time, my 10-year-old sister was ignorant of the fact that this was Cyril's idea of a pickup line. Growing up, I had watched strangers meet and become more than friendly while enjoying cocktails at my father's restaurant, so I knew a come-on when I heard it.

"We live in New Zealand," she replied, "but we're from America."

This mention of the United States clearly intrigued our dining companion.

"I love the U.S.A.," he said, putting down his plate long enough to give a double thumbs-up.

"Rocky, Rambo, Superman, Chuck Norris," he rambled off. "Tough guys. I'm a tough guy."

He flexed his impressive biceps, no doubt built up from an extreme exercise regimen of chopping wood, carrying 50-pound sacks of flour from the supply boat, and helping build *bures*.

Josephine wasn't impressed or interested. "What kind of animals do you have around here?"

Cyril must have been used to getting more attention from the local ladies for his Mr. Universe routine because his face fell. Then he brightened. "Let me show you something."

For some reason, Jo's stranger-danger alarm wasn't blaring at top volume like mine. She started to get up, but I put my arm out.

"I'm not sure Mom and Dad want you to go alone," I chirped up, partially out of annoyance that I was being treated as if I were invisible and partially out of genuine concern. It was one thing for me to give Jo a hard time – that was my birthright as her brother. This didn't mean I wanted her to get into trouble. Despite our spirited sibling rivalry, I felt protective of her, especially when we found ourselves at the ends of the earth.

Cyril gave me the evil eye but managed a tight smile. "You can come along if you want."

I knew Jo wanted to see whatever Cyril had in mind, and I was interested myself. "Cool."

I tapped my mother on the shoulder, interrupting what sounded like an in-depth discussion of cassava preparation.

"Hey, Mom, Cyril wants to show us around," I said, pointing him out. "We'll be right back."

For once, she didn't throw up a concerned excuse for us to stay put. "Fine, but don't stay away too long."

Though I would have expected this response from my father, the laissez-faire approval was unusual for my mother. Dad embraced a devil-may-care approach, then she winched him back onto more pragmatic ground. It was a yin-yang relationship that seemed to work for them even though it sometimes put them at odds.

Now was not one of those times of philosophical head butting. Moving away from the feasting, Cyril led us between two *bures* to the far side of the settlement. The grass here was uncut, rising half a foot high in a shaggy green mat. Our guide prowled ahead of us, half bent over as he peered down at the ground in front of him.

"What're you looking…," Jo started before Cyril whipped around and theatrically shushed her. He put his pointer finger to his lips, turning back to his survey with a solemn mien. From that point on, we crept forward on our tiptoes like three little Indians stalking dinner.

I kept my eyes on the ground, wondering what we might be looking for. There was nothing out of the ordinary, just unkempt lawn. Our light-footed prancing continued in silence for so long that I felt like I was waiting for the final bell to ring before summer vacation. Suddenly, our point man halted abruptly. Josephine almost stumbled into him and I nearly piled onto both of them.

Cyril was pointing just a few feet to our left. Nestled in the grass was the biggest toad I had ever seen. Probably a foot long from snout to tail, it had rough skin with raised brown splotches. Its big eyes didn't even blink; it just stared off into the distance. If I hadn't been able to detect the gentle inflation and deflation of its midriff, I would have thought it dead.

Jo let out an unconscious, "Whoa."

The creature didn't stir. I couldn't tell whether it was studiously ignoring us, quietly measuring us up, or didn't believe we were a threat.

"Cane toad," Cyril quietly told us. "Big guy."

Walking around to the far side, Jo crouched down on her haunches next to the toad. Tilting herself forward, she leaned over the inert amphibian. It would have been only natural for her to reach down and pick up the toad, like all the other exotic fauna she had fondled the world over.

Before she could give it a hug, carry it back to the dinner to show off, or whatever she had in mind, Cyril put his hand out.

"Don't touch it," he warned. "The skin is poisonous."

"Oh, okay," Jo begrudgingly relented.

I could tell that some part of her still wanted to pick it up, but her sense of self-preservation triumphed. She's lucky that it did. I later read that the creature excreted a chemical called bufotenin. Taken on its own, it could be a mild hallucinogen. This had probably led more than a few visiting stoners and experimentalists to lick the toads, hoping for a cheap LSD alternative. Unfortunately, the animal's natural defense system also produced bufotoxin, a lethal drug that sent many trippers on a permanent vacation.

At the time though, we didn't know how close we were to death. God bless ignorance and naiveté!

We watched the toad for a few more minutes, then Cyril seemed to grow bored with playing zookeeper.

"Let's go back," he said. "We don't want to miss the kava ceremony."

"The what?" I inquired as we trudged back toward the merrymaking.

"It's a good time. Lots of dancing. Maybe you'll dance with me, Jo-suh-feen?" He pronounced her name with careful deliberation, clearly trying to get it right and potentially further impress her in the process.

"Sure," she agreed with the blitheness that normally accompanies that phrase when one is responding to something trivial, like a waiter asking if you'd like more water. I mentally crossed my fingers that unmarried young women in Fiji didn't enter into some sort of marriage contract when they waltzed with a suitor.

Back at the feast, the women were cleaning up, while the men were decamping into a large *bure* nearby. Cyril joined this exodus but not before gravely promising to seek my sister out later.

My father didn't notice that someone twice Jo's age was showing an inappropriate interest.

"It's kava time," my father announced. "Noel was just about to tell us about it."

"Drinking kava is a sacred ritual here in Fiji that helps us celebrate big events," he began, before graciously adding, "Like when we have honored guests."

Clenching his fists, he placed one on top of the other and began moving them up and down vigorously, which made him look like he was strangling a child about my height. "We take the *yaqona* root – kava – and pound it into a pulp in the *tabili*. You'll see that in a minute – it's like a mortar."

He pushed downward hard as if drowning a resistant kitten. "We put the kava in a cloth bag and submerge that in a *tanoa* full of water. That's the bowl that will be at the center of the *bure*. We keep adding water till we get the right balance. It has to be just so."

We all nodded sagely, like he was a French chef explaining how the perfect proportion of lemon juice brings equilibrium to a Hollandaise sauce.

"We drink it out of a coconut shell called a *bilo*." He tilted his head back and mimed chugging. "Usually we go all night long."

Shaking his hips like a rum-drunk hula girl to finish his display, he gave us a grin. "Are you guys ready to party?"

"Absolutely!" Dad agreed without consulting the family or pausing to consider that perhaps my sister and I were on the youngish side to be raging until sunup. I was a little worried but mostly intrigued by the idea of this Fijian fiesta.

We were ushered into the *bure*, where everyone was sitting cross-legged on woven mats. Noel indicated that we should sit to the left of the *tanoa*. Carved from dark wood, the three-legged, foot-and-a-half-wide bowl – like a primitive, squat Tripod from *The War of the Worlds* – seemed to be filled with muddy water. An older man with a face so deeply lined that it looked like it was collapsing in on itself had his wrinkled hands wrist-deep in this unappetizing-looking liquid. He was massaging a cloth bag stained the color of day-old coffee.

I experienced a sinking feeling. "Is that the kava?" I asked, trying my best to sound inquisitive rather than squeamish but failing.

Noel chuckled. "Don't worry. It tastes better than it looks."

That's an easy promise to make, I thought. *It looks like raw sewage!*

As we settled in, my father could barely contain his excitement. "Now this is an adventure! Here we are in the middle of the South Pacific participating in a kava ceremony. I wish I had brought my camera. Do you think I have time to run back to our cabin and get it?"

"I don't think that would be appropriate, Ralph," my mother said. "Let's just enjoy ourselves tonight and mentally take pictures for our memories."

He harrumphed but didn't make a move for the door. Any further debate was halted when the men on either side of the kava bartender began clapping out a slow, steady beat with cupped hands. Conversations quieted as everyone else joined in. However, the clapping stopped as suddenly as it had started.

The officiant stopped manhandling the sack of kava pulp and solemnly began uttering his opening remarks in Fijian. Everyone sat respectfully while he talked, no one moving more than an eyelid. This went on for a few minutes before he stopped, clapped three times, and dipped a polished coconut-shell cup into the murky mixture. He offered it to the man on his left, who replied "*Bula*" and gave a deep, resonant clap before accepting it. Holding the wooden cup with both hands, he tipped it up to his mouth and drained it in a single sip.

The group muttered something in Fijian and gave three quick appreciative claps, which the drinker echoed after he handed the bowl back to the master of ceremonies.

This ritual was repeated with the man sitting two spots to the left of the primitive mixologist. Then the kava dispenser filled up the *bilo* and offered it to my father. Dad had the good sense to mimic the previous recipients, giving a hearty clap and an enthusiastic "*Bula!*"

He couldn't leave it at that though. Hoisting the cup above his head, he inexplicably added the Spanish toast "*Salud!*" before quaffing the contents.

To his credit, his smile never wavered, though there was an involuntary tightening around his mouth and a long pause before his Adam's apple confirmed he had swallowed. When the procedure was repeated with my mother, she looked as if she were enjoying a fine prosecco, though it took her two draughts to empty the coconut shell. Our hosts nodded appreciatively, clearly pleased with these reactions.

What came next was a surprise. I expected that the bowl would next be offered to the guy sitting next to me, but instead, I suddenly found myself presented with a bowlful of kava. My parents didn't intervene, probably concerned that my refusal would be considered a grave social slight.

Not wanting to offend our hosts myself, I gave a clap, uttered the greeting, and gingerly accepted the bowl.

I didn't dare look down at what I was going to drink, figuring that the best approach would be the same as when a Vanuatuan boy climbs to the top of the land-diving tower: Don't stop to stare; just do it. I brought the coconut shell to my lips and tipped the contents into my mouth.

The gritty mixture hit my palate with all the grace of a downpour sluicing into a storm drain. The taste wasn't much different from dirty ditchwater either.

Stopping myself from reflexively spitting it out took a monumental amount of will, but somehow I managed to swallow the kava in a single gulp. I quickly found out that there's a numbing agent in the root. My tongue began to lose its ability to taste anything and started to feel like a leaden extremity resting on the floor of my mouth. I hoped the anesthetic qualities of the kava wouldn't wear off anytime soon, since the inside of my mouth was still coated with gag-worthy grime.

Handing the vessel back and giving three quick claps, I could honestly say, "Thank you."

As in, "Thank you for getting this coconut shell as far away from me as possible!"

Josephine drank her kava with equal aplomb, though we exchanged a glance afterward that affirmed my belief that neither one of us would be ordering kava instead of Coke the next time we dined out in Fiji.

The coconut shell made its way around the room until everyone had a chance to knock back a rooty dose. Then the cycle started all over again. When the *bilo* reached my father for seconds, he raised his hands in surrender. "I'm saving room for another one of those Fijian beers!"

The rest of us demurred silently but smiling. Let's just hope that one drink was enough to satisfy the social conventions of Fiji.

With us out of the way, the scene turned into a speed-drinking contest as our fellow tipplers began to overindulge on overdrive.

Outside the *bure*, darkness fell, so several filament bulbs strung across the rafters above us were turned on, adding a vintage sepia tone to the festivities unfolding around us.

As the coconut bowl made the rounds, the light seemed to evolve. Whites became tans, tans became browns, browns became blacks, and blacks became nothingness. I found myself fixating on the hidden folds of darkness, trying to divine what was hidden in those cloaked nooks and crannies.

I wondered what monsters were lurking just out of sight. Maybe there was a cloud of the island's indigenous flying foxes hanging in the eaves just waiting to swoop down and peck our eyes out. Or perhaps a demonic iguana with a forked tongue and machete-sharp claws was skulking in the corner with mayhem on its mind.

The more I thought about what might happen, the more possibilities I imagined. I didn't know what was coming, but I knew it was coming. And it was going to make a beeline for us.

Years later, when I smoked my first joint during freshman orientation week at Vassar, I experienced something similar, though I didn't draw the connection between the two events at the time. In both instances I was there but not there. I was imagining possibilities that were really impossibilities. I was beyond the moment in my own little sphere of existence.

In other words, I was stoned out of my noggin.

I clearly wasn't the only one. Many of the Fijians looked like they were watching movies projected just a few inches in front of their faces. They were happily zoned out and enjoying the show. Clearly, they didn't know about the fleet of flying foxes hanging in the eves about to turn this *bure* into Pearl Harbor.

By contrast, the rest of my family seemed surprisingly sober if unsure of what we were supposed to do next. Not wanting to talk out of turn or disrupt the festivities, the four of us just sat there, a pale island in a sea of burnt mahogany.

The scene shifted after our fellow partygoers hit their fourth cups of kava. Suddenly, someone hit "play" on a small boombox and what I assumed was Fijian dancehall music filled the small space. Half the crowd rose to their feet with the herky-jerky grace of undead puppets; the others remained seated, demonstrating the kind of full-body lethargy that's usually reserved for heroin addicts. Those standing began to dance, weaving between their motionless companions with surprising dexterity.

This seemed the perfect cue for us to leave, but my father was having none of that – not when there was an authentic experience like this one to be embraced.

"*Arriba!*" he shouted as he jumped to his feet, pulled my mother up, and began dancing. Not wanting to be trampled by his enthusiastic exertions, Josephine and I both clambered to our feet.

Not knowing what exactly to do – and possessing all the grace of a dying gazelle stuck in quicksand – I simply began to shuffle in place hoping with all my heart that I wouldn't stand out. Josephine seemed much more comfortable with the situation, employing her years of ballet classes to execute a series of flawless twirls and complicated dance steps.

Cyril kept his promise and darted across the room like a puppy that has heard the can opener. He had clearly been imbibing plenty of liquid courage, not that his bravado needed bolstering. Upon his arrival, Josephine graciously began dancing with him. In contrast, his dance moves were somewhat spastic, somewhat fluid – perhaps an unintended precursor to twerking. The two of them formed an incongruous couple in the center of the madness.

Luckily, I wasn't a third wheel for more than a minute before a local girl took pity and partnered up with me. I didn't think she had been drinking because she possessed an astounding sense of rhythm. Her hips swayed back and forth in such a bewitching manner that it took my entire upbringing to keep my eyes focused on her face. The red floral print on her dress seemed to be shifting in time to the music, whether that was from the kava or her skills as a dancer, I'll never know.

It didn't seem like there was ever a pause between the songs. They drifted one into the next, a continuous stream of island beats, Tropicalia melodies, and exuberant choruses. I kept moving, never stopping, never talking, just letting myself get lost in the weird magic of it all.

The music was still going when my parents drifted over, sweaty and smiling, to collect us.

"I hate to break up happy couples," my father shouted over the din, "but it's time for bed."

I blushed so deeply that my cheeks took on the hue of a crimson hibiscus in full bloom. Only my father could manage to embarrass me twice in a single sentence. First he implied we were boyfriend and girlfriend, then he made me out to be a child who couldn't handle staying up all night long with the real adults. Nice work, Dad.

My dance partner didn't seem to be offended. She gave a small smile and a slight wave, then turned her back and swayed away. I stared after her. "Goodbye," I offered, but she couldn't hear me.

Cyril separated from Jo with less grace. It was more like watching a barnacle being scraped from the side of a ship as he implored her with his hands joined in prayer, "One last dance, Jo-suh-feen. Just one. Just one."

"Maybe next time, Cyril," said my mother, interjecting herself between them and putting her arm around Jo's shoulders to pilot her out of the *bure*.

Our reunited family steered our way through the dancers as Cyril called out from behind us, "Goodbye, Jo-suh-feen. I will never forget you."

We could still hear him yelling his farewells as we stepped from the hot-boxed hut into the cool evening air. Unlike the ominous blackness inside, the darkness outside was soothing, a gentle blanket covering the world around us.

Staring up at the stars as we walked back to our lodgings, I lost myself in the sparkling belt of the Milky Way. It seemed to be lit up more brilliantly than I had ever seen it before. Stretching from one end of the sky to the other, it was the definition of majesty. Peering deep into the glittering veil, I imagined a million worlds, each one full of promise.

Catching the Travel Bug

[Tonga & Western Samoa 1987, Age 13]

My mother looked down at the thermometer and shook her head. "This isn't good, Nenne."

Talk about understating the obvious. I was huddled on a paper-thin mattress soaked through with sweat that reeked of a sharp metallic tang. Despite my mother toweling me off frequently, my skin stayed persistently damp and clammy. I couldn't stop my teeth from chattering, making me sound like a manic typewriter. I ping-ponged between wanting to wrap myself in every blanket in the room and wishing I could plunge into a bathtub full of ice.

No solids had passed my lips for more than 48 hours. I had been subsisting on water and the occasional glass of ice-cold ginger ale. This was by far the longest I had ever gone without eating, but I wasn't hungry in the slightest.

"What is it?" I croaked, not really wanting to know the answer.

"103," she replied with a worried sigh, then added, "Point four."

I had no context for this response. "How bad is that?"

"You're nearly five degrees warmer than you should be."

The door opened and Dad walked in. "How is he?" he asked my mother before turning to me. "Are you feeling any better?"

"No. Not really." I tried to smile, but it felt like my lips were melting off my face. I'm sure it looked equally attractive.

"You're talking. You'll be fine," he assured me, which was not necessarily comforting since my father had always been impervious to sickness. He didn't seem to understand the debilitating effects of common colds, the flu, or anything else that didn't require a pedal-to-the-metal ambulance ride to the emergency room.

I got the distinct impression that he didn't believe that illnesses like this were anything more than attention-seeking ploys. Dad understood big-ticket ailments – an arm lost to a shark while snorkeling or a broken leg earned by land diving off a rickety tower in the middle of the jungle – but nothing else was worth acknowledging.

Clearly, my current condition didn't merit any fussing over. "So when can we leave for the other island, Alison? Do you think we can make the afternoon ferry?"

There was a long pause as my mother's jaw dropped to the floor in slow mo. It took her a moment to pick it up again.

"Are you crazy, Ralph?" she asked him in the same tone that she used when she chastised me for doing something particularly ill-advised, like trying to launch a rocket out of my bedroom window or build a bonfire in the basement. "Just look at your son. His fever is off the charts. We need to get him to a doctor. Now."

* * * * *

I should have known this trip would not be an easy one. Our journey had begun several weeks earlier in Tonga, where we spent several days in the capitol of Nuku'alofa and on the outlying island of Pangaimotu.

Along the way, I had contracted what we originally thought was food poisoning. Maybe I had eaten some undercooked chicken or a few shellfish that weren't up to snuff. Whatever it was, it was brutal. Unconsciously rehearsing for my 21st birthday many years later, I vomited heavily and promptly passed out. Waking up the next morning, I felt much better. Though I lacked energy and had the pallor of a bleached sheet for the ensuing 24 hours, we wrote the incident off as an unfortunate bump in the road.

Now we were less than 200 miles to the north of Tonga in Western Samoa. This was all part of the epic game of South Pacific hopscotch arranged on the fly by my father. We had flown into the capitol city of Apia on the northernmost side of the island of Upolu. Its architecture bridged two eras. There were charmingly weatherworn wooden structures built before the first half of the 20th century and there were dull concrete structures from modern times that housed government offices, shell corporations, and the bank accounts of tax evaders.

This leg of the trip started out calmly. We spent a morning visiting Robert Louis Stevenson's home, Vailima, perched on the hills just outside Apia. The head of state now occupied the *Treasure Island* scribe's well-appointed mansion, so we were unable to peruse the author's considerable library or see if the damask tablecloth given to him by Queen Victoria had survived the passage of time. Nonetheless, we were allowed to wander the lawns and stop in a nearby gift shop. There, I purchased several postcards and a copy of *Catriona*, Stevenson's virtually unknown sequel to *Kidnapped*, which he had penned while ensconced in this South Seas hideaway.

That afternoon we had gone in search of the sliding rocks, a series of natural waterslides that shoot extreme-sports enthusiasts over the edge of waterfalls. Despite driving in a series of ever-widening circles through the Samoan countryside, we didn't discover anything more interesting than a succession of coconut plantations, which was about as exciting as finding hayfields in upstate New York.

"Is that the only thing they grow around here?" my father grumbled as we passed the fourth palm-dominated stretch of farmland.

The question was rhetorical, but my mother nonetheless flipped open her ever-handy guidebook. Unlike my father, she actually read them before we headed off into the unknown. "It says here that coconut is one of the chief exports," she lectured, "along with bananas and vanilla."

I secretly wished we could somehow survive on those items alone. The food had been uniformly dreadful. The day before, we had picked up baguette sandwiches in town to enjoy for a picnic lunch next to the half-open air, half-subterranean Piula Cave Pool. However, when we unwrapped the white paper around the hoagies, the deli meats were so slimy, the cheese so beyond its expiration date, the vegetables so wilted, and the bread so stale that we all tossed our lunches to the fish lazily gliding through the water. Our finned friends didn't bite. The majority of our lunch simply sank to the bottom untouched.

A few mornings later, we were heartened to see pancakes on the menu at a small café and promptly ordered them. Josephine and I had a fondness for flapjacks. Every Saturday morning, my father would be in charge of cooking breakfast. His menu had two options: pancakes or waffles. I loved both choices and not just because he excelled at them. I saw both as an excuse to pour on as much maple syrup as the plate would hold.

I couldn't get enough of the dark amber liquid, but I was picky about it. When I was younger and we were living in the far western reaches of New York state, my father had built a sugar shack, tapped sugar maples on our property, and produced syrup. His maple syrup had set a high bar in my book. High-fructose corn syrup colored with caramel dye wouldn't cut it. I needed the real deal or nothing at all.

Unfortunately, real maple syrup hadn't made its way to Western Samoa. Our waitress plunked a label-less, battered bottle that was only identifiable as Aunt Jemima because of its blunted teardrop shape. When our breakfast arrived a few minutes later, we learned that the recipe for pancakes hadn't made the oceanic crossing either. Each plate featured a pair of extremely greasy deep-fried discs still sweating leftover oil from the fryer. They looked like ugly cousins of the delicious johnnycakes we had eaten in Vanuatu.

"Enjoy," the waitress urged us while we all delayed taking a first bite in her presence by fussing with our silverware, readjusting our napkins, and taking unnecessary sips of water.

My mother stalled with a question. "Do you have any jam? Maybe papaya or mango?"

"We've got something even better," the waitress responded confidently.

She returned quickly with a jar of Smucker's grape jelly, clearly sure that we would be impressed by this modern condiment. My mother graciously accepted the ectoplasmic purple spread with a resigned smile.

"I have fond memories of Concord grapes," she said as she put down the jelly and made no move to open it. "When you were born, Nevin, your grandmother came down from Massachusetts to visit us in the hospital. She hopped on a train when I went into labor and got there just a few hours after you were born."

As she reminisced, the "pancakes" leaked what smelled like rancid tuna, probably because they were prepared in the same deep fryer as the fish filets. I would have listened to my mother read a dishwasher manual in order to further postpone eating them.

"In my mother's bag was a glass quart jar of homemade Concord grape juice," she continued. "It was the first thing I had tasted for hours. I don't know why, but that juice was perfect. As I was drinking it, I was thinking, 'This is what my body has been craving.'"

"I can tell you," my father chipped in, waving his fork over his plate, "my body has definitely not been craving these...*things.*"

It was clear that none of us wanted to eat the *things* in question, but neither of my parents seemed to have a graceful exit strategy. Thank God for Jo.

"I'm not feeling good," she declared, daintily folding her paper napkin and pushing away from the table. "Can we go back to the hotel so I can lie down?"

"Of course we can," my father replied with gusto. "Check, please!"

Because of meals like this, our days wavered between ravenous hunger, as we sought to find semi-serviceable options, and the slight queasiness that ensued after we had finally eaten. It was a highly disagreeable seesaw ride.

Our only respite was the fresh fruit, which was plentiful though not particularly filling. Over the course of the trip, I ate several times my bodyweight in bananas, passion fruit, and pineapples. Beyond that, I was completely out of luck when it came to exploring what the local dining scene had to offer.

Ironically, one of the most exciting parts of this trip had not been any kind of investigation of Western Samoan culture. Instead, I had become fixated on the popular Hollywood blockbusters that were just making their way to the South Pacific on well-worn VHS tapes. My parents had made the philosophical decision not to have a television in our home, and we rarely went to the theater, so movies were a very special treat.

One of the few films I had already seen – aside from the *Star Wars* trilogy, which remained my favorite flicks for several decades – was the first installment in the James Bond series, *Dr. No.* My mother had been hesitant to introduce me to 007's world. She didn't believe that brute violence, colonialist overtones, and scantily clad women were appropriate for a child my age.

Luckily, my father overruled her, so I got to ogle Honey Ryder in her bootylicious bikini over and over (bless the creator of the rewind button!). Sure, the gadgets were cool and I re-created the fight sequences endlessly with my sister as a stand-in for a SPECTRE hatchet man, but that sexy swimsuit took the cake. Actually, it took the whole bakery.

Samoans seemed to be equally big Bond buffs. Every evening, after the local guitar quartet had finished strumming lulling native numbers, the hotel staff wheeled out a giant television set with a bulky VCR below it. I became ridiculously excited when I discovered that the first night's selection would be *A View to a Kill.*

I had read all of Ian Fleming's books at that point, so I usually knew the basics of the plots before I watched the films. However, *A View to a Kill* wasn't a part of the official oeuvre. It was conceived in Hollywood, long after the author had passed away from a heart attack brought on by the kind of relentless smoking and drinking that gave Bond a winning edge.

Around eight o'clock, after darkness had fully fallen, we settled into reclined beach chairs to take in the movie. Josephine and I nibbled on M&Ms that we had discovered in the dusty import section of a small grocery store that afternoon. My mother opted for a glass of fresh pineapple juice, while my father tucked into his second gin and tonic of the evening.

Though my opinion of the film would change later in life, I was wowed the first time through. It had all the components of a Bond classic – from Duran Duran's thrilling theme song and Grace Jones's ass-hugging leather pants to Christopher Walken's cold, calculated portrayal of the megalomaniacal villain Max Zorin.

The next night, we were treated to *Goldfinger*. I had read that book, so I knew what was coming. Not that I could ever be truly prepared for a movie that awesome. My mind was blown. There was a naked woman painted gold, a hat-wielding henchman, and quick comebacks galore. "Do you expect me to talk?" our hero asks as a laser creeps toward his crotch. "No, Mr. Bond, I expect you to die," the villain replies. Classic.

And then there was Bond's car – a silver Aston Martin DB5 – packed with amazing gizmos and futuristic weaponry courtesy of the cantankerous Q. Though the car could slash tires, shoot an oil slick out its back, and deploy a smoke screen, its ejector seat – which Bond uses to dispose of an unwanted gun-wielding passenger – was the coolest feature by far. I was pretty sure our family Volvo didn't come loaded with that option, but I made a mental note to double-check when we got home.

I was still fixating on the gadget-laden car the next day when we all piled into our rental to make a trip to an outdoor market perched on the edge of town. As I looked out the window, I imagined deftly dispatching legions of bad guys with the touch of a button. I must have looked like I was daydreaming because my father took note of my uncharacteristic silence.

"What are you thinking about?" he asked.

"James Bond's Aston Martin," I replied, still a little lost in my reverie. "It was *so* awesome."

"That was pretty cool."

"I just wish I had a car with an ejaculation seat," I said.

Dad didn't miss a beat. "So do I, son. So do I."

"Ralph!" my mother reprimanded before turning to me. "It's *ejection*, Nevin."

I nodded distractedly as I looked through her at the shifty-eyed baddie I was visualizing in her place. He had a gun pointed at my head, but I wasn't worried. With a flick of the button hidden in the gearshift, he was going to rocket into the sky.

Maybe someday, I would have my own car with an ejaculation seat that I could use whenever I wanted. I made a mental note to ask Santa for one in my upcoming annual request letter.

The market turned out to be worth the drive. It was a football field-sized concrete block covered with a rusty aluminum roof. There were orderly aisles lined with rough wooden stands, though many merchants simply displayed their goods on the ground or on faded squares of blue tarpaulin. Most vendors offered up the basics, like produce or seashells, which were arrayed in handsome, eye-catching rows that had my father stopping every few feet to take a picture.

There was a homey, casual atmosphere. Mothers nursed children openly, while others slept on mats with their kids curled up next to them. Families gathered around plates and pots, digging into communal dinners. Home and office were deeply intertwined here.

Reaching a stall that specialized in hand-carved wooden wares, I stopped to check it out. There were outrigger canoes with dapper little paddles and one-dimensional palm trees emblazoned with the phrase, "Hello From Sunny Western Samoa!" However, it wasn't this stereotypical tourist fodder that piqued my interest.

"Look, Jo," I tugged at the shoulder of her sundress. "They have kava bowls."

Peering down intently, she seemed confused. "Are they for dwarves?"

She was right. The vessels couldn't have held more than a shot of kava, but there was no mistaking the hand-hewn bowls.

"You're right, Cyril could polish that off in one sip."

That earned me a sharp kick to the shins.

It turned out that Cyril had been more persistent in his pursuit of my sister than any of us would have guessed. A few months after we returned home to New Zealand from Fiji, the first of a flurry of torturously lovesick and stiffly formal handwritten letters began arriving. Josephine's long-distance admirer outlined how much he loved her, how much he longed to see her again soon, and how much he would like to one day build her a *bure* where she could bear many children for him. When I read the letters, all I could think was, "You know she's still a child herself, right?"

At the end of his notes, he would always write, "Hello to your parents and greetings to Navel." For that, I disliked him even more.

Not that Jo was at all interested. She brushed off his advances with a casual grace by thanking him for the letter and then outlining for him in tedious detail a typical day in the life of a 10-year-old. Despite my sister's less-than-romantic accounts of horse-riding lessons, the latest furniture additions to her dollhouse, and the results of her forays into the art world (this week: vegetables made of Fimo clay!), Cyril surprised us all by continuing to court her tenaciously.

One of his lovelorn letters included a photograph of him, bare-chested and rubbed down with coconut oil, flexing in front of a palm tree. This Chippendale-of-the-South-Seas look didn't help him in his quest to win over Josephine. Nor did it inspire her to send him a reciprocal pic, which he was clearly hoping to receive. I'm sure it was a disappointing day in Fiji when he opened her response to find only a dainty letter that made no mention of their upcoming nuptials. I imagined his cartoon rage as he tore apart the envelope in a vain search for a Polaroid that would never be.

Perhaps as a way to keep bringing up Cyril, I purchased one of the small kava bowls. The merchant wrapped it up in a page of the local newspaper, the cheap ink smearing on the thin paper in long sooty streaks. Mom daintily picked up my purchase between her thumb and pointer fingers, pulled out a plastic shopping bag – which she apparently carried around for moments just like this one – and deposited the potential stain creator into it.

Meandering further along in the market, the scents of fresh-baked bread, steamed vegetables, and roasted meats awakened my hunger. A part of me refused to believe that anything we ate would be any good, but another part remained unflaggingly optimistic. Dad was always a glass-half-full guy when it came to fishing. The way my father saw a potential for angling triumphs in an algae-covered puddle of a pond, I imagined award-winning meals coming out of rundown, out-of-the-way eateries.

One stall offered young coconuts resting in well-used coolers full of ice. It seemed like a good place to start assembling an a la carte lunch.

"I'm thirsty, Dad. Can we get one?"

"How much?" My father asked the vendor, pointing down at a coconut with an overly exaggerated look of excitement on his face intended to convey his interest in buying it.

The round-faced woman with a charming gap between her front incisors made a peace sign. "Two *talas*."

My father reciprocated with his own peace sign. "Two, please."

Turning back to my mother, he gave a grin. "I bet this would taste good with rum in it."

Mom rolled her eyes but still gave him a small smile so as to not completely deflate him. Meanwhile, the stall keeper had pulled out a coconut dripping with cold water and tiny flecks of ice. Holding it in her left hand, she whipped out a machete and gave a series of lightning-fast slashing hacks to its conical peak. With a sharp tug, she wrenched off the top, revealing a small hole in the shell underneath. She popped in a straw and handed it to me.

Grasping the natural flagon with both hands, I inhaled a long slug. Slightly sweet and lightly coconutty, the ice-cold refresher was nothing like the virgin piña coladas that had become a mainstay of our tropical vacations. At first I was taken aback by the lack of a sugar rush, but after a few sips, I found myself enjoying its restrained, refreshing flavor.

With beverages in hand, we perused the lunch options nearby. My mother bought a paper plate full of freshly fried breadfruit. "It tastes kind of like French fries, Nevin."

I took a bite to find the crackly golden surface yielding a soft, starchy center that was too bland for my taste.

"Could use some ketchup," I observed, putting the unfinished piece back on the plate. "Some salt, too."

Luckily, the next stall we happened upon was offering steaming bowls of *palusami*, a local delicacy made with taro leaves, tinned corned beef, and plenty of coconut milk. The flavorful mash was easily the best thing we had eaten the entire trip, so we dug in ravenously like a group of castaways who have finally been rescued after months floating adrift. Within a couple of minutes, our plastic forks were clacking against each other as we battled for the final bites. Dad gamely bought a second round, which was hoovered up with almost equal speed.

Properly sated, we continued our amble through the market. At every food stall, my father would stop.

"Coffee?" he would ask hopefully.

If the response was positive, the vendor would then mention either Maxwell House or Folgers. This was supposed to act as reassurance that they were offering only the best, but instant coffee was anathema to my father. He would screw up his face reflexively while trying to instinctively smile politely. These contrasting emotions mashed together to create an awkward expression that horrified the Samoans on the receiving end of them.

"I'm not quite sure why they don't have good coffee," my mother wondered aloud after one disappointing stop. "I can't imagine that the Europeans here are fans of instant coffee. You'd think that some enterprising expat would open a little café."

"They'd get a lot of business from me," my father agreed. "I'd pay good money for a proper espresso right now."

No matter where we were in the world, Dad was always on the lookout for a café where he could get a quality caffeine fix. Like most of his fishing attempts in cesspools so clearly devoid of life that even a blind angler would skip over them, these java-obsessed scavenger hunts often ended in failure.

Every once in a great, great while, his quest would be successful. When presented with a worthy espresso, my father would embrace the moment like God had just handpicked him for the Rapture. He would begin by pointing out the necessary elements of the perfect espresso experience.

"Look at that froth," he'd instruct before joyfully wringing his hands. "Oh, and there's a twist of lemon on the side. That's how we used to serve it at Martell's."

Dad was a three-sugars kind of a guy, whether it came in lumps, packets, or loose. If it was the last, that meant a three-second pour from the dispenser or a trio of heaping spoons from the sugar bowl. He'd lightly stir it in, wipe the cup rim with the rind – "It adds a nice flavor" – and then daintily tip back the tiny cup for a first taste.

If the contents met with his approval, he would smile, give a nod, and polish off the espresso in short order.

"You have to drink it hot," he'd say. "There's nothing worse than a cold espresso."

Occasionally, he would offer me a taste, but I didn't understand the appeal for a long time. Though I appreciated the sweetness, the bitter bite at the end left me scrambling for a glass of water or a soda to wash away the taste. I finally came around to his way of thinking my freshman year of college, when I began craving the jolt that a quadruple-shot espresso could provide to a student pulling an all-nighter (or recovering from a sundown-to-sunup bender).

The market in Western Samoa lacked an espresso machine, much less any real coffee, which left my father harrumphing and my mother commiserating as we drove back to the hotel. Spirits were lifted when we happened upon a young boy outside the lobby who was selling leis made with the white, star-shaped *tiaré* flowers. You could smell the aromatic flora down the block, a heady tropical perfume that epitomized the South Pacific's reputation as a lush Garden of Eden.

"For you?" the boy asked my parents as we approached, holding forth an arm draped with half a dozen artfully executed leis.

My mother slowed to examine his wares. "They're beautiful," she told him with a genuine smile. "How much?"

"Four *talas,*" he replied. "All handmade."

"I can see that," Mom replied as she delicately lifted one to look at the expert craftsmanship. "We'd like four."

Digging into her purse, she sorted through the coins and well-worn bills to find the right combination. Finding exact change after a minute of peering intently at the denominations, she handed it over to the young vendor, who double-checked her math before tucking the currency into his pocket.

He gently took four leis off his arm. "I love you," he told us with such a sweet tone that it felt more like a genuine statement than a polite pronouncement at the end of a sale.

Still, it was a little odd. Anywhere else it would have been downright creepy. Imagine your butcher dropping that line as he handed over a pound of ground chuck or the mailman using it as he delivered a package. You would probably call the proper authorities as soon as you were out of earshot. But here in Western Samoa, it seemed sweet, heartfelt, and totally normal.

Donning our new accessories, we headed back to our rooms.

Everything seemed to be going swimmingly, until I woke up the next morning. I felt awful. I felt like I had gotten the flu after being run over by a Mack truck – twice – and beaten up by the gang of thuggish Cobra Kai from *The Karate Kid*. My parents let me stay in bed, hoping that some rest would clear up whatever was afflicting me. It didn't.

For two days, I slowly deteriorated. I lost my appetite, my fever spiked, and I alternated between sweating uncontrollably and feeling chilled to the core. While my mother nursed me, my father researched what we might do next on our vacation. After talking to a complete stranger over cocktails, Dad decided that heading over to the neighboring island of Savai'i would be our best course of action.

He came back to our hotel room to share his latest madcap scheme, and that's when my mother put her foot down. "Are you crazy, Ralph? Just look at your son. His fever is off the charts. We need to get him to a doctor. Now."

There was some grumbling from my father, but he dutifully headed back out the door in search of help. After consulting the front-desk staff, the local physician was called. He arrived at our room an hour later, carrying a beat-up leather bag that I assumed was full of medical equipment. The accessory was nothing but a façade; the case was empty. My exam was conducted almost entirely with the doctor's hands. He touched my forehead, took my pulse, and felt my tonsils.

"Ah," he said, tapping my right tonsil lightly. "This is it."

"Inflamed," he told us matter-of-factly. "The other one isn't much better. It's tonsillitis."

My mother nodded, like she had suspected as much all along, and gave me a comforting pat on the shoulder. Dad was all business.

"So how do we treat it?"

"There's not much you can do. Ampicillin, rest, and liquids."

This didn't faze Dad. "Can he travel?"

"Where are you going?"

"Just over to Savai'i."

"I suppose so," the doctor answered with a shrug. "There is a doctor on the island, in case he gets worse."

"Just one?" my mother chimed in.

The doctor picked up his empty bag. "Only one with a degree."

This was good enough for Dad. "I'm sure he'll get better as soon as he starts taking the antibiotics, Alison. I'll go to the pharmacy now to get the acetaminophen."

"Ampicillin, Ralph," my mother corrected.

"Penicillin. Got it."

My mother collected herself like a volcano trying to choke back an eruption. "Am-pi-cil-lin," she said slowly and deliberately. "Don't bother trying to remember it. I'll write it down for you."

Then she turned to me. "Are you up for this, Nenne?"

Her expression seemed to say, "I support you, no matter what the decision."

My father's did not. His shamelessly screamed, "If you don't get on that ferry, I will be supremely disappointed in you."

Clearly, my mother didn't feel like she had a choice in the matter. I'm sure the thought of being left behind with two children – one of them ill – while my father gallivanted around Savai'i didn't sound like a safe or sane course of action. Not that heading into the unknown with said invalid was much more appealing. At least we would all be together if I expired prematurely.

Although my only real aspiration in that moment was to stay

passed out face first – preferably on a king-sized bed not stained with my own sweat – I couldn't bring myself to let down Dad. No matter how crazy his adventures were, I still wanted to be a part of them. I was so weak that I could barely make a fist, but I somehow managed to give the lamest, limpest thumbs-up ever.

That faint sign of approval was enough for Dad. "We're going to Savai'i!" he exclaimed before overplaying his hand. "Three cheers!"

No one cheered, not even Dad.

The ferry was supposed to leave in just a couple hours, giving us precious little time to pack up and track down my medicine. The family split up along natural lines of division: My father went off alone in search of a drugstore while the rest of us gathered our belongings at the hotel.

Packing my bags felt like drowning in quicksand at night; everything was in slow motion and I could only half-comprehend what was going on. If it hadn't been for Jo's help, it would have taken me several days just to pack my bathroom kit.

I don't remember reuniting with Dad or the trip to the ferry. We may have walked. We could have taken a cab. We might have been flown to the dock by a neon pink zeppelin piloted by a talking hippopotamus for all I know.

I do know that we made it onboard the ship just as the crew was about to pull up the gangplank. Weaving our way through the cabin around various bits of cargo, we found four seats close together and took up residence. Most of our fellow passengers promptly proceeded to nap for the duration of the two-hour trip. At least that's what I was told when we docked and I was awakened from my own siesta.

I was groggy when we disembarked in the port city of Salelologa. I wasn't sure whether that was due to the fever, the drugs, or the undeniable fact that Savai'i was a little on the weird side – maybe all three. Passengers from our ferry passed by hauling all manner of objects – 100-pound bags of flour, outboard motors, and battered suitcases held together with bungee cords. Walking through the port felt like I was passing through the Mos Eisley of the South Pacific.

When we located the half-metal, half-wooden bus that would get us to the hotel, a sturdy man with a giant silver coin embedded in his stretched earlobe helped load our bags. If he had been wearing an eye patch or a red kerchief, I would have sworn he was an honest-to-goodness pirate. He turned out to be the driver and a far more gentle soul than I had originally guessed. Above his driver's seat he had a floral-fringed sign that read, "The world is beautiful when you have love in your heart."

There were two seats near the front, which Dad and I took, and a pair in the back, where Mom and Jo plopped down. We were far enough away from each other that we couldn't talk without shouting, so I leaned into the window and promptly fell back to sleep.

Occasionally, the bus would hit a bump, jarring me awake. In 10-second increments, I caught flashes of Savai'i. There were huge swathes of pandanus leaves – looking like tapered short swords made of emerald – and brown cacao beans drying in the sun on well-used plastic sheeting. A man carrying a gigantic snake tied to a pole slung over his shoulder walked on the side of the road with the nonchalance of a Sunday stroller. I couldn't tell if the monstrous reptile was dead or alive and was glad that I wasn't close enough to find out.

Many of the homes I saw were simple *fales*, rectangular wall-less huts with rounded ends and peaked roofs covered in a thatch of dried sugar cane leaves. With long stretches of near-white sand and plenty of palm trees offering shade, the beaches were enticing. Even better, they were empty.

Unfortunately, our hotel wasn't nearly as inviting. It looked like its heyday was some time in the beginning of the century. Since then, no one had bothered to keep on top of its basic maintenance. Paint was peeling off the walls, the shrubs in the yard were overgrown, and weeds sprang up between the cracks in the walkway leading to the front door.

There was a small library – if you could call it that – located just off the main lobby, where Josephine and I went to amuse ourselves while our parents checked in. The shelves were mostly empty except for a pitiful collection of seven ripped-cover paperbacks and a quintet of raggedy, waterlogged magazines that looked like they were from the 1950s.

"What is that?" Jo asked, screwing her face up into a look of utter disgust while covering her nose as soon as we walked into the room.

The scent was piercing, a combination of deep musk and spoiled vinegar with a dash of state-fair Porta-Potty thrown in for good measure. It was a gag-worthy mixture that made my eyes water.

"Ugh, I don't know." I lifted my shirt to cover my mouth and nose. "It's awful."

At that moment, a mangy-looking calico tabby scooted in between us. Normally, Jo would have instinctively gone to pick it up, stroked its matted fur, then run off to look for some kitty-appropriate sustenance. Maybe she was in a fog from the offensive odor, but she didn't move. Instead, we both watched as the feline made a beeline for the shelves. It leaped up onto the second level, took up a position at the center of an old issue of *Life*, squatted slightly, looked me straight in the eyes…and began to pee.

That was enough for me. I didn't want to repeat the vomiting portion of my Fijian fishing trip. "I'm out of here."

Jo was right behind me as I rushed back into the lobby, which was much more welcoming since there were several windows open and an overhead fan working overtime.

Looking up from perusing a pamphlet that was so old that Gutenberg probably personally printed it, Dad caught sight of us. "How's the library?"

"Skip it," I advised.

Once our room keys had been obtained, we stepped over to the hotel's modest restaurant, where I enjoyed chicken cooked in aromatic coconut milk. It was the first solid food I had eaten in three days. Although my stomach still felt unsure about accepting anything, what little I could get down tasted divine. For once, I took a pass on dessert.

As soon as we got up to our room, I fell asleep and didn't wake up again until the next morning when the sound of my sister running an ocean's worth of water roused me from my deep slumber. When she heard me stirring, she popped out of our tiny bathroom.

"Feeling better?"

"I think so." I rubbed my eyes and shook my head back and forth to see if the movement produced any negative symptoms. It didn't. Then I realized I was hungry. My appetite has always been my health barometer, so I knew I was on the mend.

When we went over to Mom and Dad's room, they were both happy with my progress.

"I knew it was nothing," my father crowed, even as my mother filled a glass of water so I could take my next dose of ampicillin. "You're a trouper."

Mom was more circumspect. "I'm going to keep an eye on you for the next few days. I don't want you swimming or straining yourself until you're all better."

"But I really, really wanted to go snorkeling," I protested with a grimace.

She was unmoved. "You can't always get what you want."

Now that I was in my mother's care for the day, she was taking no chances. There may have been some poor choices made getting us to this point, but she was doing her best to ensure that no more were made going forward.

Downstairs, the continental breakfast buffet was limited but nonetheless substantial. I helped myself to fresh fruit, a bowl of Raisin Bran, and a glass of pineapple juice.

"Where's the meat?" my father kvetched as he poured himself a cup of what was promised to be coffee, though I was pretty sure it was nothing more than instant sludge. He took a sip. His grimace confirmed my guess. As he grumbled under his breath, he added three sugars and a healthy splash of milk, clearly hoping to drown out the brown water's unnatural flavor as much as possible.

It was average fare, but it all tasted fine to me – until I happened to overhear a conversation unfolding at the table next to us.

"I swear to God, Erma, that rat was the size of a dachshund," exclaimed a portly older gentleman wearing a faded polo shirt that strained at his midsection and a navy blue captain's cap with a golden anchor embroidered on it. I put down my fork to listen further, my appetite suddenly stalled.

The speaker held his hands two feet apart. "It was this long. And it was in our bathroom."

"Are you sure you weren't dreaming, honey?" the woman, whom I took to be his wife, responded while easing a triangular morsel out of a halved grapefruit. "You did have two glasses of wine before you went to bed."

There was a thump and the clatter of flatware as the complainer pounded the table like an infant demanding dinner. "I wasn't drunk, if that's what you're implying," he retorted. "I know the difference between a real rat and a figment of my imagination."

He took a swig of his coffee and then continued. "If I was going to dream about something, it would be about one of these sexy Samoan girls."

Clearly, his wife had been putting up with such proclamations for eons because it didn't seem to faze her in the slightest.

"I'm sure they're dreaming about you, too, dear," she

condescendingly cooed. "Isn't it every woman's fantasy to run off with a 72-year-old former used-car salesman from Wisconsin?"

That shut him up, but it didn't clarify to me whether or not I should expect our room to be invaded by giant rodents that night. I made a mental note to make sure no sheets were hanging off my bed so the beasts didn't have anything to climb up.

After breakfast, my father broke from the group to investigate the fishing possibilities. That left the three of us to explore on our own.

"Let's go down to the beach," my mother suggested. "The sun will be good for you, Nevin."

With a thick layer of sunscreen applied and my fanny pack around my waist, we trotted down the road, through a small stand of palm trees, and onto the sandy expanse that edged the South Pacific. The water was postcard perfect, a vibrant teal in the shallows that transitioned to a rich blue farther out.

Peering first down to the left and then to the right, I realized that we were the only people on the beach. The tide was going out and the high-water mark was littered with plenty of shells. I split from Mom and Jo and began nabbing the best ones, along with smooth-cornered translucent pieces of sea glass, which my mother collected and displayed at home in a large bowl on our coffee table.

As I walked along, I thought back to Honey Ryder's entrance in *Dr. No*, as she strode out of the surf in her head-turning two-piece. I surveyed the ocean wistfully, hoping to spot a snorkel that would then reveal a curvy starlet. I wasn't in luck. First no ejaculation seat, now no Bond babe. Life just wasn't fair.

Turning despondently toward the tree line, I spotted a rectangular mound of sand ringed with carefully arranged empty beer bottles. Flowers sat on top of the sandy knoll, while colorful cloths flapped in the wind above it on bamboo poles. There were other manmade hillocks similarly adorned just beyond it. After a moment, I realized that these must be Samoan graves.

That evening over dinner, I told my father about the gravesites.

"They sound beautiful," he replied between bites of lemon-buttered fish filets and steamed taro. "I'll have to get over there with my camera. I had an intriguing day myself."

When my father said "intriguing," I always steeled myself for what came next. Usually that meant that he had discovered a place, person, or activity that most sane, reasonable people would view with suspicion since it usually led to half-cocked adventures with varying degrees of danger attached to them.

"I met a wonderful German guy named Helmut," my father continued. "He was paddling by the dock in his dugout canoe with his dog."

This last fact piqued Jo's interest. "What kind of dog was it?"

Dad wasn't interested in a sidebar discussion. "It was brown. Anyway, I'm going out with him tomorrow. He tells me that the fishing around here is the best he's ever done."

There was no arguing with Dad when he was in angler mode. The next day, we went down to the beach again while he went adventuring. While we were adding to our shell collections, we saw Dad and his new fishing buddy paddling out to sea. I wished I had a camera; the two of them would have made a poignant photo.

Helmut was at the aft of the dugout paddling vigorously next to a mangy mongrel, whose name we later learned was Cha-Cha. My father was at the prow – paddling with surprising energy and coordination – his head turned toward the horizon like he was the lookout. I followed his gaze – there was nothing to see but bright shards of sunlight glancing off endless ocean.

When Dad returned late that afternoon and met up with us on the beach, it sounded like he had spent the entire expedition drinking Helmut's Kool-Aid.

"Whatta guy," my father testified with stars in his eyes. "Helmut's a real pioneer. He moved here from Germany a decade ago after retiring from the Merchant Marines. Married a nice Samoan girl, and they have a son. They live just down the road. You'll get to meet them all – we're having dinner over there tonight."

Jo and I exchanged a roll of the eyes. I'm sure Mom was thinking about giving hers a spin as well, but she was usually far too restrained and polite to give in to the temptation. Though she was a child of the Sixties, my mother had been raised by somewhat conservative parents who placed a premium on manners and decorum.

"I'm sure it will be lovely," she murmured.

My father nodded vigorously. "I'll have to ask him about the process for moving here. I wonder if it was difficult. Don't you think it would be so amazing to get a hut on the beach here?"

Jo and I exchanged another look, this one more alarmed. Before my mother could answer, Dad barreled on.

"Just think, Nevin, we could go fishing every day," he exclaimed like he was fantasizing about how to spend lottery winnings. "I could get a little boat with an outboard motor and leave it tied up at the dock. No lock required! Who's going to steal it? It's an island!"

I refrained from pointing out that the item in question was a seafaring vessel so not putting a lock on it wouldn't prevent someone from hopping into it and absconding with it to a different island.

He was working himself up into a *One Flew Over the Cuckoo's Nest-*worthy froth. His eyes were gleaming as he stared off into the distance at a future only he would want to imagine. "God, it would be so wonderful. So simple. So easy…."

He trailed off, his gaze still locked at some point a few years down the road. My mother took this pause in his monologue to inquire after a few practical elements that Dad clearly wasn't considering.

"It's definitely an idea," she began graciously, employing the kind of phrase that sounds amendable but actually doesn't mean anything. "But where would the kids go to school? Would you really want to be on an island with one doctor? How would we survive without good coffee, Ralph?"

I couldn't tell if the last question was serious or if it was intended to be a dash of humor to offset her more serious inquiries. Keeping Dad grounded was part of her job, but she clearly relished it as much as being told she had to pop all the balloons at a kid's birthday party. In both situations, chances of a tantrum were well over 100 percent. Dad didn't let her down.

"Why do you always have to be so negative, Alison?" He glared at her petulantly. "Look around. We're in paradise. Who doesn't want to live in paradise?"

"I'm not saying it isn't gorgeous, Ralph."

Jo and I began edging toward the door. Whenever my parents began punctuating sentences with each other's name, it meant that an argument was brewing. For good or for ill, they made a point of trying not to fight in front of us. Those fiery exchanges were saved for behind closed doors when they assumed we were in bed. I still heard them quarreling late at night sometimes, but I preferred sleeping to eavesdropping.

"I'm going to go identify the shells I found," I offered to a point somewhere in between the two of them without making eye contact with either one. "Jo's going to help me."

My sister nodded vigorously, causing her brown hair to bounce like she was trampolining.

"We'll see you later," she offered as I cracked open the door just enough that we could slip out.

Neither Mom nor Dad verbally acknowledged our departure, but I did hear my father restart their testy tête-à-tête. "Why can't you ever embrace an adventure, Alison?"

"Maybe because moving to Western Samoa isn't an adventure, Ralph," Mom shot back. "It's a fool's errand."

Back in our room, I pulled out Robert Louis Stevenson's *Catriona* and propped myself on a few pillows at the head of my bed.

The book begins with a dedication to some guy named Charles Baxter: "It is the fate of sequels to disappoint those who have waited for them." Stevenson clearly had never seen *The Empire Strikes Back*.

Jo flopped down on the single bed next to mine only to stare up at the half-hearted ceiling fan slowly spinning in uneven circles that barely moved the air. I thought she was going to just let me quietly enjoy my own book and escape the family feud for a little while. I wasn't that lucky.

"What do you think it would be like to live here?"

I kept reading, hoping that my silence would cut the conversation off before it began.

Apparently, my lack of a reaction meant that I was contemplating an answer, so Josephine filled the void with her own thoughts on the matter. "It would be really nice to live next to the ocean. You could go snorkeling every day."

I grunted noncommittally.

"I wonder if they have horses here? Or maybe I could bring one from New Zealand, so I could keep taking riding lessons."

She clearly wasn't going to let this go. I sighed dramatically before giving up the pretense of reading and putting down my book.

"You'd better hope they have horses here because there's no way Mom and Dad are going to pay to have one shipped in. That would cost a lot of money. Like probably a year's worth of allowances."

"Why would I need money?" Jo fired back. "There's nothing to spend it on."

Fair point, but I wasn't going to let her win the argument. I changed tack.

"Imagine what Christmas would be like down here," I said and then began ticking off a list of downsides. "No snow. No snowmen. No snow forts. No snowball fights. No sledding. No hot chocolate. No Christmas tree, unless you want to decorate a palm tree. No visits from Gramma and Grampa. Santa probably wouldn't even be able to find us out here."

I shouldn't have added that last item.

"Don't be silly. Santa can find anyone anywhere," Jo replied. She was right. He had found us no matter where we lived – New York City, Pennsylvania, and even New Zealand.

This was not going as smoothly as planned. When Jo wielded logic against me, I resorted to the nuclear option. "Can't you see I'm trying to read, dumbass?"

She stuck her tongue out at me. "Whatever. Just admit that it might be interesting."

* * * * *

Interesting was certainly the first word that came to mind when we all showed up for dinner at Helmut's house that evening. The structure was more Eastern Bloc than Western Samoa with a cinderblock foundation, plywood walls, and rusty corrugated-tin roofing. In keeping with local custom, there was a doorway but no door. Light spilled out from the interior, revealing a pair of feral cats licking open sores in the dust by the steps.

As we approached, my father sang out *"Guten tag, comrades"* in an over-emphasized German accent that wouldn't have been out of place in a Monty Python skit.

"Hello. Come in," replied a voice from inside.

Entering the house, we found ourselves in a small living room. Helmut was sitting at a stubby-legged Formica table next to a young boy with caramel-hued skin and brilliant blue eyes.

Our host stood up and waved toward the boy. "This is my son,

Fedor. Fedor, come meet our guests."

My father made introductions, and we all exchanged formal handshakes. In the midst of it all, Helmut's wife walked in from outside smelling of smoke and cooked meat. A dome of tightly curled dark hair topped off a round face bullseyed by a slightly flattened nose and a broad mouth spread even wider in a welcoming smile. She introduced herself as Afiui, which set off another round of handshakes.

"What are you cooking?" my mother inquired. "It smells delicious."

No matter where you go in the world, chefs love that compliment. Western Samoa was no different. Afiui gave Mom an appreciative nod. "It's the fish your husband caught and some lamb. Would you like to see?"

Another universal truth about chefs: If they want to show off what they're working on, you never deny them the pleasure.

"We'd love to," Mom rejoined as if she were reading from a Miss Manners script. "Come on, kids."

The three of us trotted back outside behind our hostess, who brought us over to a small stone-and-dirt barbecue. Smoke was belching from its depths like a dragon working overtime. There was a pile of dried-out coconut husks on the ground next to the cooker. Afiui lifted the piece of worse-for-the-wear corrugated tin roofing on which our dinner was cooking and shoved a few bits of this kindling into the blaze.

Mom was right – it did smell inviting. However, dinner didn't look that appetizing. There were vertical score marks on the midsections of the day's catch, but they seemed to be otherwise untouched by any culinary handiwork. Fat from the lamb flaps, otherwise known as the belly, was dripping into the dips of the makeshift grill like the aftermath of a grease storm.

"I bet that lamb is going to be really baa-d," I quietly quipped to Jo, who stifled her giggle in clenched hands.

100

Luckily, Afiui didn't hear us. She was more concerned with turning the meat over with a pair of flame-kissed iron tongs, which looked they might have been used for torture sessions back in the Dark Ages. My mother either chose to ignore our exchange or was too focused on her mental calculations on whether the fire was hot enough to kill any bacteria that lurked inside the dead flesh that was to be our dinner.

Satisfied that everything was proceeding as it should, Afiui ushered us back into the house where Helmut had arranged some hors d'oeuvres – ice-cold bottles of Fanta soda and a platter of Chips Ahoy cookies.

Dessert before dinner? Things were shaping up. Plus, this would allow me to fill up before we were subjected to the dodgy-looking meal that we would inevitably be forced to eat.

Dad was deep into a discussion about the local real estate scene with Helmut.

"The only question is, how much beachfront do you want?" the German dream weaver told my father in between sips of electric orange soda.

Upon hearing that, my mother turned back to Afiui and began chatting about traditional Samoan 'ie toga weaving. That left Josephine and me with Fedor. Unfortunately, we quickly realized that Fedor was bilingual – in Samoan and German – so I resorted to miming.

Picking up a cookie, I took a bite and let out a loud, contented, "Mmm...."

As if that wouldn't make my point enough, I grinned and rubbed my belly. Fedor, who must have been just a few years my junior, gave me one of those piteous smiles that is usually reserved for drunks passed out in public or people who have just managed to walk into a light post. Even Josephine was looking at me like I was a halfwit who had wandered away from his elephant cage-cleaning duties at the third-rate traveling circus passing through town.

My awkward attempts at silent conversation were put out of their misery when Afiui announced that dinner was ready. As well as the goods from the grill, she brought out a bowl of steaming rice, roughly chopped cabbage tossed in lime juice, and fried taro and breadfruit. New glasses were procured and cold Cokes were poured.

"Cheers and thank you so much for having us," Dad toasted. "Who knows, we may be your neighbors someday soon."

Everyone politely clinked glasses, then dug in. Despite my misgivings, the food was lovely. The fish was slightly sweet, light and flaky, which nicely complemented the simple slaw and starchy sides. Josephine was a big fan of the lamb flaps, devouring them voraciously.

I wouldn't mind this fare on occasion, though I couldn't imagine eating it day in and day out. I would miss the same stateside staples I'd been yearning for while living in New Zealand – New York-style pizza, Reese's peanut butter cups, and my grandmother's shoofly pie. In general, the cuisine in the Southern Hemisphere couldn't hold a candle – not even a matchstick – to the food back in America. New Zealand's prize lamb was usually so dully prepared that the gaminess was accentuated, its ketchup was sickly sweet, and meat pies were filled with a viscous mixture of over-salted gravy and fatty bits of beef.

It seemed shallow and selfish to write off an entire swath of the globe just because the grub wasn't good enough, but I had to endure Pacific cooking at least three times a day and it was oftentimes more pain than pleasure. Plus, each bad bite was a reminder of our family and friends back in the States.

After dinner, we thanked our hosts and headed back to the hotel. The road was well lit from a nearly full moon and a sky brimming with stars. We walked side by side, Josephine and I in the middle with our parents flanking us. It was a quiet night soundtracked by the rustle of palm fronds swishing in the slight breeze and the clip clop of our flip-flops on the dirt.

At first, no one said anything at all, content to digest the meal and the day. We were about halfway back to the hotel when my father suddenly began to softly sing, "This old man, he played one. He played knick knack on my thumb."

Dad's vocal work was usually limited to Christmas Eve carols and bad accompaniment to jazz standards. I couldn't remember him ever singing me a goodnight lullaby or leading a fireside sing-along on camping trips. Not that he had a bad voice. He always joked that it was his teenage years as a Catholic choirboy that gave his pipes a little shine.

Mom joined in for the next lines with her sturdy mezzo-soprano. "With a knick knack paddy whack/Give a dog a bone/This old man came rolling home."

We all sang the next verse, jubilantly adding this unlikely song to the sounds of Savai'i.

"This old man, he played two,
He played knick knack on my shoe,
With a knick knack paddy whack,
Give a dog a bone,
This old man came rolling home."

I found myself smiling in the inky blue darkness of the road. Much of my joy in that moment simply came from feeling well again. I had come to realize that there was only one thing worse than being sick: being sick far from the comfort of home.

Even though living in New Zealand somehow felt temporary – like it was just another stop on one of our vacations – we had put down tentative roots there. We had made friends, developed routines, and grown comfortable. It never felt like home as I remembered our life in America, but I had developed a deep fondness for our new life Down Under.

The idea of displacing our lives yet again to an even stranger set of circumstances here in Western Samoa freaked me out to no end. I enjoyed exploring the farthest reaches of the globe, as long as we could return to a somewhat normal life at the end of the itinerary.

Part of what made the trips so exciting was the fact that they were just quick peeks behind the veil.

Thankfully, Mom was of a similar mindset. So long as she could keep Dad's wandering ways limited to vacations rather than relocations to the wildest hinterlands, we would be fine. I shuddered to think of what might happen if that balance ever tipped too far in my father's favor. The results would be cataclysmic. I crossed my fingers that would never happen.

Do You Speak Een-gleesh?

[The Azores 1988, Age 13]

"You have a weird accent," declared the kid next to me in third-period study hall. "Are you foreign or something?"

"We just moved here from New Zealand, but I was born in New York City," I replied, extending my hand. "My name is Nevin."

"What kind of a fucking name is that?"

My handshake hung unrequited in the aisle between our two graffiti-scarred desks. I pressed on, hoping to avoid creating any kind of a scene that would attract further attention. "It was actually my great-grandfather's name."

"He lived in Pennsylvania," I added in an effort to bolster my stateside bona fides.

That tidbit didn't seem to impress my classmate, whose slender face topped with a jumbled mop of blond hair wore an expression caught somewhere between suspicion and disdain. "Good for him. I have no idea where my great-grandfather lived. Don't care either."

He addressed the rail-thin teen in a plaid shirt to his left. "Get a load of Neville over here. He's from…." he trailed off for a second. "Somewhere. Not here."

"Nevin from New Zealand," I interjected, I thought helpfully.

Both of them snickered at that.

"You're in Clinton now," the first one declared, pronouncing the town's name with a silent o – Clint'n – before completely turning his back on me to mark the end of our conversation.

So much for the power of politeness. Not knowing how to

proceed, I redirected my attention to my textbook and tried to lose myself in the story of the American Revolution. There's nothing like the tale of a small band of underdogs triumphing over tremendous adversity to pick up the spirits. However, there were a lot of losses and setbacks before we all got to binge on hot dogs every 4th of July. It looked like I was still at the Battle of Long Island stage in my own struggle, and it felt like the Battle of Yorktown might never come.

We had crash-landed in this blip of a burg in central New York a few weeks earlier. Located 45 minutes east of Syracuse, Clinton was indistinguishable from many other towns in the region. There were lots of agriculture, a ridiculous amount of snow in the winter, and generally conservative inhabitants. There were pockets of liberalism, mostly due to the town's one differentiating characteristic: Hamilton College, a small liberal arts college that added a whiff of sophistication to the town's résumé.

Higher education wasn't what had attracted my father to this small village of fewer than 2,000 souls. He had come in search of what he called "apple pie America." There was no arguing that Clinton fit the bill. A drive through the picturesque downtown area sent you past a stone Presbyterian church and old-fashioned pharmacy at one end of the village green, and a brick fire station and post office with the stars and stripes flapping proudly in front of it at the other.

On the surface, it was equal parts Norman Rockwell painting and toy Christmas village – the perfect cure-all for a homesick family that just wanted a little bit of the world that Garrison Keillor trawled through every weekend for *A Prairie Home Companion*.

According to locals, the fishing in the area was excellent – another huge selling point for my father. Perhaps it was his angling addiction that prompted him to buy a charming manse built in 1831 on the main street before even consulting my mother. When he called to tell her the news, I could tell she had mixed emotions about his initiative-taking.

Though my mother loved New Zealand and was disappointed to be leaving our life there behind, she still missed her family and friends back in the States and she was clearly relieved that Dad hadn't decided to move us all to Savai'i.

On the flipside, Dad had never felt settled or satisfied in the far southern reaches, so pulling the trigger on a new life in a new town was a no-brainer.

I was homesick for America myself. It came down to the little things – like the fact that in New Zealand it was difficult to find American comic books, Thanksgiving wasn't a valid holiday, and I had to wear itchy wool uniforms to school. Those might seem like inconsequential gripes, but it's the smallest pleasures that yield the greatest joy.

Once my father had made up our minds for us, things moved quickly. Before we really had time to emotionally or psychologically process the idea of uprooting our lives again, we had packed our belongings, bid our friends farewell, and were winging our way back around the globe just two and a half years after we had departed the States in the first place.

Despite the fact that we were moving back to the country we had grown up in, the culture shock felt like Muhammad Ali repeatedly punching me in the face. Until we'd stepped back onto U.S. soil, I hadn't known that it was possible feel like a foreigner in your homeland.

As I discovered in relatively short order – courtesy of my not-so-welcoming junior high classmates – the way I spoke, my cultural reference points, and my personal fashion sense (or lack thereof) couldn't have been more foreign. It was a little forced at first, but I quickly learned to drop my New Zealand accent (though I would occasionally forget myself and say goodbye with a hearty "Cheers, mate!"), I cut off my rattail and grew out a mullet, and I did my best to catch up on the popular TV shows, movies, and music of the day.

When summer vacation rolled around, I was relieved. Finally some time to simply relax and find my equilibrium. My father, ever the intrepid adventurer, sought no such balance. Just because we were on home soil didn't mean that his wanderlust was satiated or that our itinerant life would be predictably stable. I found this out when I moseyed into the kitchen for dinner on an otherwise uneventful Tuesday in July.

He was seated at the head of our enameled table, a double Glenlivet slowly sweating as melting ice conspired with the heat of the evening. There were several guidebooks piled in front of him, pages turned down and little bits of paper sticking out all akimbo. He was deeply engrossed in the Frommer's guide to Portugal, which gave me a brief flash of hope that we would be traveling somewhere that my classmates might be able to find on a map.

"Are we going to Lisbon?" I asked optimistically.

My father tilted the book down, looked over the top at me, and gave a perturbed shake of his head. "Why would we bother with that tourist trap?"

Without pausing from tossing the greens for a salad, my mother gently interjected, "Ralph, Portugal is actually supposed to be quite beautiful."

He didn't seem to hear her. "We're going to the Azores."

"The Aye-zores?" I pronounced the name slowly. It sounded exotic and mysterious. Then again, so did Mordor – and that hadn't been a cakewalk for Frodo and Sam.

He placed the book down on the table, spine up, and took a quick nip of scotch. "They're islands in the Atlantic, west of Portugal."

"I read this article about it," he said, hoisting an issue of *National Geographic*, its canary yellow border faded to a mute citrine. "You'll like it. It's subtropical, so your mother will be packing your snorkeling gear."

That sounded promising; my father's next answer did not.

"So, what're we going to be doing there?" I inquired.

"Who knows?" Dad said with a shrug of his shoulders and one of his the-devil-can-go-to-hell grins. "I'm buying airline tickets, renting us a car, and that's it. The plan is to go with the flow."

I could almost hear my mother's eyes rolling in rapid-fire succession, but she didn't say anything.

"Sounds like it's going to be an adventure, Dad," I offered gamely. "I can't wait to get into the water."

* * * * *

Several weeks later, I found myself looking out over the wind-kicked, froth-topped expanse of…

Lake St. Clair in northern Michigan, just outside the front door of my Uncle Willy's permanently parked trailer home.

The waters in front of me couldn't have been a less tropical tableau, but I dove in nonetheless. A long day of cramped, sedentary travel had made me itchy for activity and a shower – the lake offered a two-for-one special.

I should have looked a little closer before I jumped. I hit the water with perfect form, and my arms cut through the surface into what turned out to be a dirty swill that looked like mud when I made the mistake of opening my eyes for a microsecond underwater. Coming up for oxygen, I took in a lungful of diesel-accented air.

"How is it?" Jo yelled from the shore.

"It's great," I said, and then added, "I feel like we're already in the Azores."

As soon as I tacked on the embellishment, I could tell from her expression that I had overplayed my enthusiasm.

"Yeah, right. Nice try, dick," she turned away before calling over her shoulder, "By the way, you've got eggshells in your hair."

Clambering out of the water as quickly as I could, I discovered that she was right. Foisted on top of that indignity was the fact that it took two showers before I could shed the scent of Lake St. Clair.

We were staying with my Uncle Willy in the small town of New Baltimore to the north of Detroit. As we drove along New Baltimore's main street earlier that day, my father cuttingly, but correctly, observed, "No quaintness. No charm." It looked like it had tumbled a long way down from its 1950s heyday. Store signs were faded, and the windows were haphazardly filled with merchandise that looked four decades old. You half expected to pick up a paper and see a headline crowing the armistice that ended the Korean War.

We were passing through this depressing hamlet on a lightning fast two-day visit to see all my father's relatives who still lived in Michigan – most of them not too far from their birthplace in nearby Mount Clemens.

Uncle Willy's decidedly immobile mobile home was outside of town on one of the many canals – known as cuts – that connected to the main body of St. Clair. The shore on the other side of the lake was Canada; the one I was on was packed shoulder to shoulder with white houses sporting black-shingled roofs and sun-faded American flags flapping lightly in the breeze. This lakefront property was my uncle's one modest extravagance. For the most part, he was frugal to the point of being clinical.

"Growing up poor will do that to you," my father told me when I asked about the meticulously curated collection of Wonder Bread bags I discovered in a box under my bed. "You learn to save everything and never throw anything away."

That didn't make complete sense to me.

"But *you* don't have a box full of old bags under your bed," I pointed out.

His face softened. "I got lucky. Just remember one way isn't better than the other; it's just the way it is."

He wasn't kidding about the luck. My father was the youngest of 17 – seven boys and 10 girls – but easily the most financially successful of the bunch. He was the final pronouncement in his mother's more than two decades of childbearing. She had died – undoubtedly worn out from years of non-stop and ever-mounting maternal duties – when he was only 10 years old.

His father wasn't in the picture much, so throughout his childhood, Dad was cared for in rotation by his large pool of siblings. Willy and another brother, Ronnie, helped him at a key juncture when he was a teenager by getting him a bartending gig in Key West, Florida. That ultimately led to a long, profitable career in the restaurant industry, which peaked with the purchase of a corner property on the Upper East Side of Manhattan in 1963.

He named the place on 83rd and 3rd Martell's, though he extended the name to Martell & Son when I was born in 1974 and Martell & Son & Daughter when Josephine joined the fold two and a half years later. I liked sitting at the bar and chatting with the bartenders and the servers. When my mother wasn't keeping tabs on what I was eating, I'd always order one of the hefty burgers. They came with a side of fries, which were cut into rounds slightly thicker than potato chips so they stayed golden crisp on the outside while still possessing soft centers.

It wasn't an all-American eatery by any means. To create depth and sophistication, my father added European accents to the place – a classically trained French chef, a top-tier espresso machine, and imported mineral water (a rarity at that time).

Over the years, some of his brothers ended up tending bar for him – including Willy and Ronnie – and they would often end long shifts with hardcore drinking sessions and endless rounds of euchre, a game that was as inscrutable to me as the baccarat James Bond played before he switched over to poker. Whenever the brothers reunited, several decks of Bicycle cards would come out after dinner, along with chips, cigars, and plenty of cocktails.

"Who wants a Presbyterian?" my father would ask after a trip to the liquor store. Everyone always answered in the affirmative, usually with the directive to "pour heavy."

Ronnie would usually add a dig. "Don't stiff me like you did the last time. Was there any whiskey in that one or did you just give me ginger ale?"

No one could remember who originally created the cocktail – though Willy liked to take credit for it – but no one argued that it was their brother Dorn who named it. But why he called the combination of Canadian whiskey mixed with equal parts club soda and Canada Dry ginger ale and a lemon peel a Presbyterian, no one seemed to know either.

In a way, it didn't matter. That cocktail was part of the fabric that bound the brothers together. It was a commonality that my father continued to share with them, even as his life pursued a drastically different arc from theirs. Dad didn't seem to feel guilty about his prosperity and success, but he did make every effort to share the wealth. Whenever there was a family get-together, my father would pick up the bill for dinners, find a gracious way to stock his host's pantry, and make a contribution to his nieces' and nephews' college funds (and oftentimes his siblings' wallets as well).

Dad had been splashing out money since we arrived. Never cavalierly or ostentatiously. He just figured out a way to pay for everything. When we had gone grocery shopping for a barbecue Willy hosted one evening, my father had slyly sent his brother back into the aisles for one item while he proceeded to pay for an entire shopping cart worth of groceries. It made me realize how seriously he took providing for not just the four of us but his entire family. Just like his traveling style though, he was very carefree with this caretaking. It never seemed to be something he overthought or stressed over; it was simply something he did.

After two days partying with and pampering the extended Martell family, we boarded a flight from Detroit to Boston, where we picked up another plane bound for Terceira, the biggest island in the Azorean archipelago. From there we took one last puddle jumper onto our final destination, the city of Ponta Delgada on São Miguel Island.

As we drove into town through rolling emerald pastures spotted with small copses of trees, it was easy to see why São Miguel had earned the nickname "The Green Island." The viridian landscape found a contrast in the furrows of tilled rich red earth in the fields and the terracotta tile roofs with their distinctive spired chimneys that resembled miniature tower penitentiaries for Lilliputian Rapunzels.

Perched on the edge of the Atlantic, Ponta Delgada had narrow streets lined with dark-and-light-patterned cobblestones. Architecture spanned the past to the present, though it was the century-old buildings that were the most striking. That evening, we dined in one such spot, Hotel Sao Pedro, a boxy structure with whitewashed walls, black accents, and a renowned restaurant inside. It took its formalities very seriously, boasting servers gussied up in mock tuxedos, white tablecloths, and no prices on the menu.

"Do you speak Een-gleesh?" my father asked our waiter with a hopeful tone, before reemphasizing his inquiry. "Een-gleesh?"

The server gave an apologetic shake of his head. "*Não. Eu falo português.*"

This gave my father a moment of pause before he charged forward in broken Spanglish. "What are the *las especiales* of the day, *señor?*"

Despite my father's grave syntactical errors, his question seemed to register. "*O prato do dia é lulinha.*"

Dad let out a long, appreciative ah. "Baby goat," he matter-of-factly announced to the table. "A specialty in the Azores."

He turned back to the server. "*Uno bebê goatee, por favor,*" he instructed with a conductor-like twirl of his menu.

The waiter looked perplexed but nodded deferentially before taking the rest of the table's orders.

My father settled back into his chair, confident and pleased with his choice. "This should be a memorable treat."

About 20 minutes later, our server and another waiter arrived with our entrees. Each porcelain plate was hidden under a silver dome. The dishes were placed in front of us and unveiled simultaneously with a coordinated flourish.

All eyes immediately zoomed in on my father's plate to bear witness to his *bebê goatee*. Our shock was collective. For unless the kitchen had decided to serve just the entrails of the goat, there was no way that the spaghetti-like confusion of tentacles was a *bebê goatee*.

For once, my father was speechless. He waggled his head like a man shaking a Magic 8 Ball in hopes of obtaining a different answer to his question. This was not the reaction our waiter had expected.

"Senhor, há algum problema?"

Still my father did not speak. Instead, he picked up his fork and began inquisitively lifting the tangled mass, looking to see if his desired baby goat was hiding underneath it. This left my mother to frantically dig into her bag to retrieve her miniature Portuguese dictionary. After a few harried moments, she arrived at the word she was looking for.

"Cabra?" she inquired, pointing at my father's dish.

"Não, senhora, é lula. É...." The waiter was clearly searching for another word that might be more explanatory to this table of clearly confused English speakers. As usual, my mother was the picture of grace, proffering him her small dictionary.

Flipping through the pages with crisp flicks, he arrived at the word he was looking for.

"Squeed."

"Squeed?" my father repeated, not understanding what I had suddenly realized was to be his dinner.

"Sim, senhor."

The light bulb suddenly went off over Dad's head. "Squid," he said with a melancholic incredulity, as if he couldn't – or at least didn't

114

want to – believe what he was saying.

Pleased that he and his customer had finally come to an understanding, the waiter gave a wide smile and a short bow before beating a hasty retreat so that my father didn't have time to gather his wits and place a new order.

For a moment, the rest of us sat there in total silence staring at my father with the kind of nervous anticipation one feels when the biology teacher drops a mouse into the snake cage. I could feel myself holding my breath because nothing ruined my father's mood quicker than a bad meal at a high cost.

The seconds ticked by – it seemed like a minor eternity. Then my father gave a half-hearted stab of his fork and speared one of the miniature cephalopods. He held it aloft in front of his face, examining it for a moment before resignedly popping a tentacled morsel into his mouth. He let it sit there, probably wishing that he was a million miles away at that moment. Mom, Josephine, and I were riveted, like spectators at a NASCAR race who are secretly hoping for a fiery collision to relieve the boredom of endless left turns.

Without warning, my father deliberately and determinedly clamped his jaws together and began to chew. Still none of us said a word. After a sturdy mastication, he paused and swallowed. I imagined the baby squid slithering down my father's throat – a one-way ticket to its own edition of *Fantastic Voyage*. The beady-eyed beast reached the first stop on the intestinal thruway, giving my father a moment of pause.

Looking up, he seemed surprised that he was the center of our rapt attention. Never one to squander an audience, he rose to the occasion.

"Tastes like chicken!" he exclaimed. "But chewier."

A few days later, my father's misunderstanding of mealtime vocabulary took another unexpected turn when we drove to the neighboring city of Ribeira Grande. The server was equally unversed in English, and my father continued to refuse to crack open the dictionary (this time my mother didn't swoop in to offer assistance). Dad again happily opted for a daily special, convinced he would be getting a veal chop. Unfortunately, it was a bluntly prepared liver-and-onions dish that my mother called an anti-aphrodisiac, though she wouldn't clarify what that meant.

As I was chuckling over my father's continued gustatory misfortune, my own dinner arrived to wipe the smirk off my face. What I had understood to be roast chicken could only have been such a thing if the poultry in question had been bred with a gnome in mind. It was about the size of a clenched fist and the golden roasted hue of a freshly minted Florida retiree. The legs were daintily tied together – if one can refer to the restraint of a dead bird's appendages as dainty – whilst the tiny wings were tucked in at its side.

"Could be a canary," my mother opined after a lengthy examination of the diminutive bird, which included peering at it from every angle and flipping it over twice.

That didn't sound particularly appealing to me. "So you're telling me that my dinner was probably bought in a pet store?"

"I don't know, Nevin. Maybe it's a local delicacy." She shot a look at my father, who either missed it or studiously chose to ignore it.

Or perhaps he was too thoroughly enjoying my discomfort to be distracted. "Where's your sense of adventure, Nevin?" he challenged. "Take a bite."

If only to prove to him that I wasn't afraid, I carefully cut off a small part of the breast and popped it in my mouth. I let it sit there for a moment, allowing the tension at the table to grow. Now everyone was looking at me, waiting for my pronouncement on my exotic entrée. In that moment, I understood my father's desire to cater to the crowd. When everyone laughs with you – instead of laughing at your name or your accent – life is a little sweeter for a second. I chewed, swallowed, and smiled.

"Tastes like baby squid," I quipped. "You know – like chicken, but a little chewier."

116

Not all the meal selections had unintended consequences. Every morning, we enjoyed a five-star breakfast delivered to our rooms, which we ate on the balconies overlooking the harbor. There were crusty just-baked rolls smeared liberally with slightly salted pats of butter and rindy orange marmalade, bowls of cubed fresh pineapple, and rounds of Gouda cheese.

Josephine and I opted for steaming cups of frothy hot chocolate, while my parents savored expertly prepared café au laits. "Finally, a decent coffee," one of them would invariably remark between sips; the other would nod silently in agreement as if a great mystery of life had been revealed.

After we were properly primed, we spent our days crisscrossing the island. As we were cutting from north to south one afternoon, we came across a small ramshackle distillery. It seemed about as legitimate as your average bathtub gin or backwoods moonshining operation. On the far side of the room, a series of steampunk-styled stills wheezed slowly and steadily, while on the other side, half a dozen aging alcoholics propped themselves up against a makeshift bar matter-of-factly crafted out of pallets nailed to the top of stacked wooden beer crates. They looked up at us, seemed to register that we were strangers – but the non-threatening kind – then kept sipping their handmade spirits.

With more than five decades of hospitality experience under his belt, my father had cultivated an uncanny ability to seamlessly become a regular in any restaurant or watering hole he entered – whether it catered to kings or paupers.

"*Hola*, gentleman," he offered as he bellied up to the bar. "What's the house specialty?"

As everyone in the place turned to watch with no small amount of interest, the bartender wordlessly produced a fingerprint-spotted jelly jar and set it down. From under the rickety counter, he pulled out a dirty bottle that still sported the gummy residue of a long-gone label. Tipping it completely upside down, he filled the glass nearly to the brim – what my father would call "four fingers full" – with a clear liquid.

He made a sharp drinking motion, as if he were guzzling it all in one shot. Dad's eyes widened slightly, but he'd been in enough bars to know that this drinking dare was the equivalent of a prison initiation. If you don't prove your manliness when they first came at you in the laundry room, you'd spend the duration of your incarceration as a punching bag.

Hoisting the glass, he toasted his fellow tipplers. "*Salud!*"

A few returned his toast. The rest seemed to be waiting for what came next. To his credit, Dad took the flagon's worth of firewater down in a single swig. If the Fijian rum was diesel, this homemade hooch was clearly napalm. His eyes bulged out, his gag reflex kicked in, and he quickly put his hand over his mouth. For a few seconds, he leaned against the rough wood of the bar, slightly bent as he fought to tame the high-proof firewater coursing through his system. Then he seemed to pull himself together, like a boxer shaking off a jaw-rattling uppercut.

"*Mucho bueno, mis amigos!*" he told the crowd, coughing heavily.

If they didn't look impressed, the other barflies at least looked satisfied with Dad's ability to stomach their rotgut. The bartender made a move to refill my father's glass, but his hand shot over the top of it with a quickness that would have made Mr. Miyagi proud.

"*No, gracias.* I need to, um…" He sputtered out for a second before placing his hands on an imaginary steering wheel and twisting them to approximate making a hard right turn. "…drive-oh the car-oh."

The bartender shrugged his shoulders, and everyone resumed socking back the white lightning. We returned to the car, my father half-staggering over to the front passenger seat, uncharacteristically giving up his commander's perch.

"Actually, you drive, Alison. I'm not sure I'm up for it."

My mother spent a good five minutes adjusting and readjusting the seat and mirrors until she was satisfied. I amused myself by reading the copy of *National Geographic* that had led us to this booze-soaked mid-Atlantic island with some dubious culinary traditions. Every once in a while, I would come across a word or phrase whose definition I couldn't define by its context. One expression popped up that I had seen before but never understood.

"What are the anals of history, Dad?"

Despite his half-drunk condition, there was no mental stutter step. "It's where all the assholes go when they die," he cracked.

My mother didn't blink, but she did take one hand off the wheel to deliver a hearty "thwack" to my father's shoulder. She turned her attention to me in the rearview mirror.

"It's the annals of history, Nevin. Ann-nahls." Her repetition of the pronunciation was even more drawn out, so she sounded like a ghost (which actually turns out to be the wicked amusement park owner) in a *Scooby-Doo* cartoon.

"It means a record of a time," she continued. "Your diaries are the ann-nahls of your life. Will you remember that?"

"I won't forget," I promised. "I'm going to write about all of this in my diary tonight. Just one question: How do you spell asshole?"

* * * * *

When you travel with my father, you have to embrace the idea of going with the flow because it's his *raison d'être*. Anything can change from minute to minute – itineraries are ever-evolving propositions, moods dip and soar mercurially, and an announcement that we would be uprooting our lives and moving wherever we happen to be visiting was always a possibility.

So it was no surprise when he told us halfway through the trip that we were shifting our lodging arrangements to a house in the country, which was owned by a woman he had just met at the airline office. Frankly, I would have been equally nonplussed had he proclaimed that he had made plans to go cliff diving at night with a man he met while knocking back a breakfast cocktail at the local pool hall.

It turned out that Ruth was one of the saner individuals Dad had ever glommed onto. Warm, welcoming, and deeply knowledgeable about the island, she lived 10 minutes outside Ribeira Grande in a generously proportioned pension. Her son, Gonzalo, who was about my age, immediately adopted Jo and I as his charges, giving us a full tour of the handsomely decorated house and the property around it. The terracotta-topped two-story sat on a sizable chunk of land, which included several overgrown pastures fringed with forests.

"Lots of birds live there," he said, gesturing toward the leafy groves in the distance. "All different kinds. Some only live on São Miguel Island."

This factoid intrigued my Dr. Doolittle of a sister, whose enthusiasm for all creatures great and small came rushing out. "I love birds. I used to have a parakeet named Poll. Do you ever get to pet them?"

"No," Gonzalo replied pointedly. "I shoot them."

Jo's face fell, and for just a second, I thought she might actually cry. "Why would you do that?"

"The museum in town pays good money for the rare ones. We eat the others." He shrugged his shoulders noncommittally, as if to add, "It is what it is." "Do you want to see the long-eared owl I killed?"

On the rare occasion I was presented with an opportunity to remind my sister that she was younger – and therefore wimpier and weaker than me – I took it.

So even though I wasn't sure I particularly wanted to spend time with a cadaver, I said, "Sounds cool. Let's check it out."

He led us out to the back patio, where the lifeless corpse bathed in warm sunshine it could no longer enjoy. Though it was smaller than I expected – just over a foot long – I imagined that in flight, swooping out of the night sky to pluck a field mouse scampering through the long grass, it had been majestic.

Dimmed discus eyes set in black-rimmed half-moons bisected by a white V of fur led down to a sharply hooked beak. Its wings were tucked down at its side, much like those of the roasted canary I had eaten a few nights earlier. The feathers were an attractive motley of brown, black, and buff with hints of white. You could have mistaken the owl for merely sleeping if you overlooked the neat splash of crimson on its breast.

Lying there in repose, it reminded me of the mahi-mahi my father had caught in Fiji. One minute, these creatures were nonchalantly proceeding through their lives when – bam – they became someone else's trophies.

Hunting for dinner was a messy business. I hadn't warmed to the thrill of the kill, despite the countless fishing trips. Maybe it was because our expeditions always ended with my hands covered in guts, blood, and the fish's undigested last meal as I artlessly fileted our catch.

Though I recognized that death was an inevitable component of sustaining life, I preferred it to happen in slaughterhouses and barnyards far removed from the dinner table. A pig wasn't a pig – it was pork. Just like a cow was beef and a chicken was poultry. It wasn't until years later that I overcame this wimpy worldview. Now when I look at a haunch or a filet on my plate, I take a moment to thank the creature I'm about to eat for its sacrifice – then I devour it. I'd never want to work in an abattoir, but I'm no longer squeamish about where the meat that I eat comes from or what's required to get it from the field to my fork.

Josephine interrupted my philosophical reverie. "I don't want to look at this poor owl anymore. I'm going back inside."

In that moment, I felt like I should underscore that I was the more mature of us. I did this as only a bratty, graceless 13-year-old can. Which is to say, completely immaturely.

"What's wrong with you? Can't handle a little death?"

Why I felt the need to be so condescending and insensitive to my little sister, I could not tell you to this day, but that's the nature of siblings. No matter how much you love one another, there's always an element of sadistic competition. Over the years, we had our fair share of rivalries and dustups, but they usually didn't venture into such cruel territory. Looking back, it was not my finest moment.

Josephine didn't even bother responding; she just turned her back and slowly trudged back to the house. Gonzalo and I stood there for a few more moments, wordlessly looking at the owl, until he felt the need to break the silence.

"I could take you hunting tomorrow," he offered. "Maybe you could kill a bird, too."

What Gonzalo thought was a generous offer put me in the most awkward of positions. I really had no interest in making a contribution to a local ornithologist's collection by taking down a bird I would much rather watch in flight. However, I didn't want to disappoint my host or reveal to him that my show of manliness was just a performance. Robbed of its intended audience, it now proved to be little more than a flimsy façade concocted to belittle my sister.

"Sure, sounds great," I heard myself saying. "Just don't tell my mom. She would totally flip out if she knew I was using a gun."

Gonzalo gave one of his little shrugs. "No problem. We'll go early in the morning before anyone else is awake."

That night, I couldn't sleep soundly. Whenever I drifted off, I'd find myself in the middle of the same nightmare over and over again. I was running through a field of towering tall grass, which made it impossible for me to see in front or behind me. As I roughly brushed up against the flaxen shoots, it sounded like a parchment flipbook being roughly scanned. My feet thudded against arid earth, and my breaths came quickly and raggedly. I knew I was being chased, but I didn't know why.

Just when I felt like I had escaped, I'd suddenly feel a breeze on my neck. Turning around, there would be a pair of golden eyes dive-bombing toward me from the blackness above. I would scream – a high-pitched squeal worthy of a morally loose high school cheerleader getting knifed in the opening act of a horror film – which would jolt me awake. I'd find myself sweating profusely with the covers on the floor and my sister staring at me from her bed across the room.

At first she asked concerned questions – "Are you okay? Do you want some water?" – but by my fourth rude awakening, her queries had taken on a more annoyed tone. "What's your problem? What kind of wimp freaks out over a dream?"

By the time the night sky began transitioning from blackness to gold-kissed deep blue, I was mentally and physically exhausted – and dreading the hunting expedition even more.

True to his word, Gonzalo lightly tapped on our door just a few minutes later. We stealthily made our way through the quiet house. Just outside the backdoor, his small rifle with a brown leather strap rested against the wall. It had a wooden stock with a stubby scope attached to its dull black barrel.

Though I had seen plenty of guns in James Bond flicks, in the living re-creations at Valley Forge, and strapped to banana republic militiamen, I'd never been in a situation where I could actually shoot one. That inspired a number of mental queries, none of them particularly optimistic: Can ammunition spontaneously explode? What if a bullet ricocheted off a rock and hit me in the eye? How would my mother kill me if she found out I was using a gun?

Slinging the firearm casually over his shoulder, Gonzalo lead me through a field filled with a golden grass that looked eerily similar to that in my dream. The only difference was that I was tall enough to see over the gently swaying sward, though it occurred to me that if I were reincarnated as a field mouse – typical fare for an owl – I'd be getting the same perspective I had experienced in my dream. It wasn't a comforting realization.

To take my mind off my thoughts, I quizzed my safari guide, who responded with the shortness of a Hemingway character.

"So how'd you learn how to hunt?" I began.

"Uncle."

I tried a new tack. "What's the biggest animal you've taken down?"

He shrugged. "Rabbit."

"Does it ever bother you when you kill an animal?"

"Why?" This was accompanied by a look that seemed to say, "Why are you asking this stupid question?"

I pressed on. "Have you ever accidentally shot someone?"

This inspired my pathfinder's longest answer.

"Not yet."

As I prayed that I wouldn't be the first victim of a slip of the trigger, we arrived at a copse of trees that stretched from where we stood over the top of a hill probably half a mile away. Gonzalo put his finger to his lips and began moving forward on the balls of his feet. I fell in step behind him, trying to avoid the twigs and pinecones littering the ground, which could alert wildlife that there were intruders in their neighborhood. I thought of Hawkeye from *The Last of the Mohicans* stalking Magua through the Adirondacks, though I wasn't hell-bent on rescuing a comely colonial lass.

For a few minutes, we proceeded in total silence as Gonzalo scanned the canopy above. His head swiveled slowly back and forth, sometimes pausing for a moment to stare intently at a spot in the leafy bower before continuing his survey. Upon reaching a clearing, he put his small hand across my chest, stopping me in my tracks.

Pointing across the way, he singled out a cedar tree and jabbed toward its upper reaches. Obviously, there was something up there, but I couldn't see it. All I could make out was an unremarkable tangle of branches and leaves. I tried looking away and then returning my gaze to where Gonzalo was gesturing. Still nothing.

My guide didn't have much patience. Soundlessly moving behind me, he pointed past my eye, so I was looking down his arm like it was the barrel of his gun. Following the tip of his finger into the natural camouflage, I realized that one of the patches of leaves wasn't like the others; it was a gray pigeon. It wasn't an owl, but Gonzalo didn't seem to care. Nodding to let him know I saw it, I wasn't sure what came next.

The rifle suddenly appeared before me as Gonzalo hoisted it over my head. For a second, I stared at it like it was an alien life form. Tentatively grasping the barrel with my left and the stock with my right, I held the gun in front of me for a moment. There was a well-worn patch on the butt where it had rested on the young huntsman's shoulder. In my hands, it was smaller than it looked but sturdy.

With another insistent poke of his finger, my guide dropped back and left me standing squinting across the way at the blissfully ignorant pigeon. Did Azoreans actually eat them? When we visited New York City, Dad always called them rats with wings. I couldn't imagine a situation where I would ever willingly eat one of those filthy rodents, unless it was the only sustenance I could catch when stranded on a desert isle.

Maybe he planned to sell the corpse to the local museum? However, I couldn't imagine they would want something as ordinary as a wood pigeon. That left me wondering whether I would simply be participating in a sport killing. I was already squeamish about the thought of plugging this pigeon, but I knew my conscience would simply not let me do it for fun.

No matter how I felt about the situation, I knew how Gonzalo felt. For him, the pigeon was a target, not a philosophical debate.

I could feel him watching me, judging my hesitation, and downgrading his estimation of me. Slowly, I raised the rifle to my shoulder, just like I'd seen it done in the movies. Angling my head downward, I peered through the scope. Now the pigeon was easy to spot – a glaring gray blip against the green foliage. The white patch on its neck stood out like a bullseye. My prey looked completely unworried, occasionally cocking its head as if listening for a call from a friend.

The black crosshairs stood out sharply against the small bird's chest. I tried to slow down my heart, which was attempting to jackhammer out of my chest. I checked the crosshairs one more time, took a deep breath and squeezed…my eyes shut.

I have never wanted to do anything less, but I knew I couldn't bear the shame of not doing it. Pulling the trigger, I heard a crack and felt a small kick from the gun.

I languished for a moment longer in the darkness. I didn't want to open my eyes to find the pigeon with a bloody hole in its chest. I didn't want to have to carry its limp corpse home. I didn't want my sister to resent me. I just didn't want the responsibility of having unnecessarily taken a life.

Gonzalo interrupted my self-recrimination. "You missed."

I slowly cracked open my eyes. The first thing I saw was my hunting companion, staring at me, a look of disdain growing as it crossed his face. I could feel my cheeks turning red as shame coursed through me. Not shame for my apparent weakness, shame for being caught wallowing in perceived cowardice.

"I think your scope is broken," I muttered.

"Sure," he said dismissively, his eyes never leaving mine.

There was never any pretense that we would overlook my inability to perform and continue hunting. Instead, we plodded back the way we had come in complete silence. I had no more questions, and he clearly didn't want any answers from me.

I felt drained of pride and hope. My failure had grown to epic proportions in my mind and did not auger well for my chances for long-term survival in catastrophic situations. If I were ever stranded on a desert island, I would be dead within a week – and that was being overly optimistic.

No one would ever call me a modern-day Robinson Crusoe because they don't write books about guys who don't survive. They just write quick news stories about unidentified remains being discovered on a remote atoll. The last line of the article would read something like this, "Though the medical examiner determined that the unknown boy died of hunger, one of the sailors who found his body noted that the island he was on was 'rich with edible animals that he clearly couldn't kill and eat because he was too much of a wimp.'"

The worst part of the whole experience was when we got back to the house to find my sister waiting for us outside. Her eyes were puffy and her little fists were scrunched up tightly. Her small body shook as she spat her question at me.

"Did you kill anything?"

I wanted so much to tell her that I had tried but couldn't bring myself to do it. Maybe her pride in my restraint would replace her current disappointment. Through that validation, I would feel like less of a failure. Actually, there had been nobility in what I had done. It was worthy of hearty congratulations. I had held a creature's fate in my hands, and I had granted it life. I was a kind-hearted god!

"He missed," Gonzalo said as he kept walking.

I'm sure she hated me even more in that moment than she would have if I had actually killed the bird. I couldn't even do that right, but the intention was there.

"You're a bastard."

"Jo...." I trailed off. She turned her back on me and followed after Gonzalo.

I knew there was nothing I could say that would convince her otherwise, so I turned around and walked back into the field. Somewhere in the middle, I stopped. I pushed down the long stalks, and a cozy nest appeared, an island in the middle of an island. Lying on my back, my gaze followed the blonde lines of the grasses to their feathered tips and the cloudless azure sky beyond. Their musty scent mixed with wildflower pollen tickled my nose. Insects chittered and chattered. This white-noise hum was calmness incarnate.

As the sun slowly climbed in the sky, I didn't move. I lacked the courage to face my family. My cowardice was multifaceted, so I was letting everyone down in a unique way. Each person would have an individualized look of disappointment for me.

My sister was disappointed that I had tried to kill a bird. My mother would be disappointed that I had used a gun. And my father would be disappointed that I had failed to kill said bird when I had used said gun.

There was no one to turn to except myself, and I felt too lost and lonely to be able to find comfort within. I would have run away, but I knew from my performance that morning that I didn't possess the chutzpah required to make it in the wild. Not knowing where else to go, I just lay there and let my eyes get lost in the deep blue above me.

Ultimately, I finally worked up the nerve to return to the house, but only because I was ridiculously hungry. Tramping back, I steeled myself for lectures, ostracization, and punishment. When I arrived in the kitchen though, my appearance was greeted with nothing more than a "Good morning" and a "How did you sleep?" from my parents and our host. Josephine and Gonzalo remained silent. Sitting down next to my sister, I was just waiting for her to blurt out, "Nevin went hunting this morning and tried to kill a bird."

I steeled myself for the inevitable shit storm this would unleash as I reached in front of her to grab a few slices of whole-wheat toast and the bowl of jam. After all, if you're going to go down, you might as well go down with a full stomach. As I slathered my bread with an overly generous amount of strawberry preserves, I saw Jo opening her mouth.

Instead of a loud accusation though, she quietly hissed at me,

"Don't worry. I didn't tell Mom and Dad."

My surprise must have been highly obvious because she added, "I'm not a rat."

I quickly checked to see Gonzalo's reaction, and he slightly nodded. By some tacit agreement, it seemed that both were resolved to keep my secret. My shame would not grow! I knew I would never forget it, however.

"Don't forget that we're going to have a little party for your mother tomorrow night," Dad reminded us as I scarfed down my seventh piece of toast and offered up thanks to the gods above for their stay of execution. "It's her birthday."

For the next two days, we continued our survey of the island, but most of our discoveries were disappointing bodies of water. We visited the lamentably flameless *Lagoa do Fogo* (Lake of Fire), held our noses while Dad took a dip in a hotel swimming pool that smelled like a urinal, and visited hot springs that were nearly unapproachable – never mind broachable – because they reeked so badly of rotten eggs.

We laughed about the sulfur and made fart jokes as we sat down to celebrate Mom's birthday.

"It's amazing to think that a year ago, we were in Fiji," she mused between sips of champagne. "A year before that, we were on Shelter Island for the summer waiting to leave for New Zealand. The year before *that* we were living in Chadds Ford, Pennsylvania."

That didn't even include all the trips in between – Western Samoa, Tonga, a quick nip over to the Cook Islands, traveling the length of both of New Zealand's islands, and several diaries more worth of destinations that were so small that they didn't appear on most globes. So much ground, so little time. Despite all the places we visited though, we were missing a key terminus: home.

Back in Clinton, I was Neville from Somewhere-Not-Here. When we traveled to far-flung locales, I was Nevin from Not-There. It was hard to find stability and form lasting relationships while bopping from one side of the globe to the other. I was hesitant to make friends, worried that I'd simply have to say goodbye to them sooner rather than later. Though I could always seek solace in a book, it sometimes made me lonely to read about friends on adventures instead of going on adventures with friends myself.

I hoped that someday, I would find a real home whose welcoming embrace and its surrounding community would always be waiting for me – no matter where I traveled in the world.

Hello, I'm Robinson Crusoe

[Trinidad & Tobago 1990, Age 15]

When you are little, you believe Valentine's Day celebrates universal love. By the time you're in high school, you realize it's a time for the world to remind you just how many people don't love you, don't care about you, and don't even want to spend the time it takes to acknowledge you exist. For many of us, Valentine's is one of the most demoralizing days of the year.

The couples are even more dry-heavingly cute and cuddly than usual – making out in the hallways with loud slurping noises, exchanging matching silver-plated jewelry purchased at the nearby mall, and showing off homemade tattoos that profess undying love while showcasing poor grammar (JE & TP LUV4EVA). Girls might give out cards and small gifts – some Necco Sweethearts here, a heart-shaped box of Russell Stover chocolates there – but they're only for their girlfriends, guys they're crushing on, or former flames. These romantic gestures definitely weren't given out to a girlfriend-less, prospect-less guy like me.

Whereas I was considered a fringe element to most of my classmates, Josephine had transformed herself into one of the popular girls. Whip smart, outspoken, and strikingly pretty, she prided herself on standing out as the belle of the middle school with the same determination that I tried to assimilate.

She was like a lightning rod, attracting admirers effortlessly. That meant February 14th would bring a cascade of cards, gifts, and proclamations of endless affection, though it wasn't uncommon for her to receive such attention on other days of the year. I envied her for this cult of personality, though I could never bring myself to say it.

So one evening when my father announced we would be leaving on the Valentine's Day of my freshman year of high school for a weeklong vacation on the Caribbean island of Tobago, I heaved a massive sigh of relief. Josephine and I never had a say in the vacation planning – even my mother's influence was minimal in this department – but for once I didn't mind.

On the other hand, Jo was highly unamused. "Are you serious, Dad?!!? Why can't we leave the next day?" she whined.

"The tickets were cheaper," he replied mildly, clearly uninterested in getting tied up in a tit-for-tat with a stormy teenage girl.

The table shook and the silverware jumped as Jo stomped her foot. "You are totally ruining my life!"

"Stop being dramatic," my mother gently interceded while washing lettuce in the sink for a salad. "You're going to love Tobago."

"Maybe you'll meet the next Cyril," I added.

Without another word, Jo clomped out the room, making sure to bump into me as she exited. "You're a bastard," she muttered just loud enough for me to hear.

"A week of this is going to be fun," I noted. "Don't forget to pack armor."

* * * * *

A few weeks later, we were winging our way across the Caribbean Sea. Carnival season wasn't set to start for another week and a half, but a contingent of our fellow passengers at the far back of the plane seemed to have gotten the dates mixed up. Even when the drink cart wasn't making its rounds, the party posse was constantly hitting their attendant call buttons to request an escalating cascade of drinks – from Bloody Marys to beers to tequila shots.

"Looks like they're ready to party," my father wistfully noted as he tucked into his own generously poured scotch on the rocks.

Mom had a more circumspect opinion of the revelers.

"I just wish they'd wait for the plane to land," she offered between sips of ginger ale. "There will be plenty of time for them to party when we're not all jammed together in a claustrophobia-inducing metal tube."

"Come on, where's your sense of fun, Alison?"

"Packed right next to the book I plan to read alone at the beach," she primly shot back. "Both will come out when the time is appropriate."

Mom would have preferred we pick just one port of call per vacation and that we took it easy once we got there. That way we could spend our time really getting a sense of the place rather than never stopping long enough to truly get our bearings. She saw our trips as an opportunity to slow life down, not speed it up.

Over the next hour, I found myself moving from Dad's perspective over to Mom's. In the beginning, the spirited shenanigans were if not infectious at least mildly amusing. It's hard not to laugh at a man dressed in a pink and turquoise Hawaiian shirt and a neon yellow Panama Jack hat – a get-up that would make even Don Johnson blush – when he dances down the aisle while singing "Margaritaville."

However, after dinner service was over, the trays were cleared, and rational souls started thinking about a nap – especially those of us who'd been up before dawn to catch our flight – the boisterous binging became more annoying than endearing. As the cabin lights dimmed, the volume grew louder. The king of karaoke was now attempting to lead his fellow partygoers in a boozy a cappella rendition of Buffett's "Why Don't We Get Drunk," but he kept forgetting the words.

"Why don't they shut up?" I griped to my father in a singsong mockery of the lead singer. "Don't they know that this is the time that normal people go to bed?"

Jabbing the attendant call button for a refresher on his drink, he shrugged. "Carnival is a part of the culture in Trinidad and Tobago. When it comes to local customs, you just have to do what the natives do. Those guys are just getting into the spirit of the celebrations."

Even before Dad had a family, he had enjoyed travel to exotic ports of call, including Mato Grosso and Havana, where he had the pictures to prove that he had indulged in local customs galore – from enjoying more than his fair share of Caipirinhas to salsa dancing.

He did an awkward shimmy and shake in his seat. "I'm getting ready to groove myself. We'll see if we can get your mother out on the dance floor."

Looking over at my mother, who was fast asleep with my sister softly snoring against her, I thought that his chances of any *Saturday Night Fever* action were probably unrealistic, but I kept my mouth shut.

A minute later, the ruckus in the back died down. I didn't care what shut up the karaoke king so suddenly. It was now quiet enough to take a nap before we landed. I offered a silent thank you, reclined my seat, and closed my eyes. Finally!

The universe had other plans. There was a crackle above us, and the pilot's voice came over the intercom system. "Good evening, folks. Sorry to wake some of you up."

Passengers began stirring and looking around in the dimness either unsure of where they were or dreading what might come. As long as the pilot's next words weren't "Fasten your seatbelts" and the plane didn't plunge toward the ocean, I felt like I was ready to handle this new wrinkle.

"Unfortunately, we have a sick passenger who needs immediate medical attention," the pilot continued. "I'm diverting the flight to San Juan, Puerto Rico, so we can get him to a doctor."

When the stewardess arrived with my father's scotch, we discovered just why we would be making an unexpected stop on the Isle of Enchantment.

"Jimmy Buffett needs to get his stomach pumped," she told us, jerking her head back toward the once clamorous choir, which was now utterly silent. "He won't be enjoying a cheeseburger in paradise anytime soon – unless they give it to him through an IV drip."

* * * * *

We arrived at Port of Spain at two in the morning, over five hours behind schedule. After waiting half an hour for my father's 80-pound bag full of fishing gear, camera equipment, and festive-themed Carnival clothing to appear on the clackety carousel, we trundled over to the airport hotel.

Face-planting on my bed without regard for undressing or brushing my teeth, I fell into a most disconcerting dream that was so odd it even stumped the therapist I later visited in my twenties.

I was floating in star-speckled space while clenching fistfuls of quarters. Brightly colored popsicles drifted by in the void, which I fed with the change like they were arcade games. Once loaded, I then used my mind to telepathically shoot the edible missiles at endless legions of stormtroopers. In the background, I could just make out Darth Vader ominously urging them, "Take him alive. No disintegrations!"

When the wake-up call jolted me out of this nightmare only three hours later, I was so on edge I flailed all my limbs to find the phone in the darkness. As I knocked it out of its cradle, I also managed to bat a pitcher of water off the bedside table, which my mother must have put there after I conked out.

Bang! Crash! "Shit!"

The clamor roused my sister in a high state of alert.

"What the hell is going on?" she yelped in the darkness. "Was there an earthquake?"

"Shut up and turn on the lights," I snapped before pulling back on my acerbic tone. "Get out of bed on the far side though, there may be broken glass on the floor."

"Only you could manage to break something in your sleep," she chided as she flipped on the light switch and surveyed my swath of

135

destruction. "Nice work."

I began plucking glass shards out of the carpet. "Bite me. Are you going to help?"

"I don't think so," she said as she flopped back down and pulled the covers over her head. "Keep up the good work, loser."

Our moods hadn't improved much by the time we met our parents in the lobby to return to the airport. There was no time to eat breakfast and the flight to Tobago was only 15 minutes long, so we didn't even get a cup of commercial-grade OJ to take the edge off. The only upside was that the engines were so loud we couldn't gripe at each other or hear our stomachs growling.

When we arrived, we piled our mountain of luggage and ourselves into a cramped jeep-turned-taxi to get to our lodgings, which were perched midway along the southern shore in the village of Belle Garden. It was a beautiful day – radiant sun, a tropical temperature, and a cool sea breeze to keep the heat in check. As we wound our way along the coastline, the rich scent of curried vegetables and stewed meats would occasionally find its way into the car to inflame my raging appetite. After the second whiff, I was more than a little curious.

"Something smells really good," I noted as I kept sniffing the air for another virtual taste.

Our driver gave a wide grin. "Roti shacks."

"What're they?" Jo wanted to know.

"Have you eaten Indian food before?" he asked in return.

We both nodded, having grown fond of samosas and curries in Fiji's capital of Suva before we had ended up over on Matangi island.

"It's like that but wrapped up in crepes." He paused. "Do you know what crepes are?"

"They're very thin, savory pancakes," my mother interjected. "I think you'll like them."

Further discussion of this fascinating new foodstuff was halted when we arrived at our final destination. Set on a gentle hill, the whitewashed, plantation-style manse stood out from the well-curated lawns and verdant jungle surrounding it. Two sets of steps led up to the front door on the second level, where the owner stood.

He had closely cropped, tightly curled hair that was just starting to gray at the temples and was dressed in khaki shorts and a white linen shirt unbuttoned halfway down his chest where a pair of glasses dangled. With a newspaper in one hand and a mug in the other, he looked every inch like a tropically accented absent-minded professor. We later found out he came to the role naturally. His full-time job – far off the island – was as a professor of African history at Columbia University.

"Welcome," he bellowed with a proper British prep-school lilt. "Jolly good day, isn't it?"

"Jolly good indeed, matey," my father hollered back in a mock English accent that sounded like a very drunk Errol Flynn, who was actually Australian. "Is it teatime yet?"

"If you'd like a cup, I'm sure I could get the housekeeper to put the kettle on," our host answered gamely.

"Actually, a cup of tea sounds lovely," my mother chirped up. "The last 24 hours have been quite draining; we didn't get much sleep."

"Terribly sorry to hear it," lamented our host. "Never fear, now you're at the Richmond Great House. You're in the lap of luxury, a sanctuary, a Caribbean Shangri-La."

Ascending the stairs, we introduced ourselves to this proprietor of paradise.

"Hollis Lynch, a pleasure," he told me as we shook hands. "Might you like some breakfast?"

We answered in an impromptu chorus. "Yes, please!"

He led us through a spacious living room ringed with packed bookshelves and decorated with African tribal masks and primitive statuettes. As we shuffled behind him, Dad's monster bag rumbling loudly on the dark hardwood floors, Lynch gave a quick history lesson on the house-turned-hotel.

"This main building was erected in the middle of the 18th century," he said. "The property was originally a sugar cane plantation, though subsequent owners moved into manufacturing sugar, molasses, and rum. After that, it became a coconut and cacao farm. I purchased it in 1973 and have subsequently done my best to revive it to its original glory."

On cue, we arrived at a spotless veranda overlooking the property and the surrounding forests that cascaded down to the sea. More importantly, there was a table pertly dressed with a white linen tablecloth and smartly arrayed with plates of sunny-side-up eggs, crispy rashers of bacon, and slices of hearty-looking whole-grain bread so fresh that it was still steaming.

For a second, we were all silent. Lynch's earlier boast was right: This was like arriving at an oasis after a dispiriting journey through the desert. Then we all lunged for seats and inhaled the food like a pack of zombies devouring an unfortunate soul.

Once sated, my parents split off from us to make a quick trip into town to pick up our rental car. Josephine and I decided to explore the surrounding property, which turned out to be a fantasyland for my budding zoologist of a sister. A flutter of squawking parrots winged upward from a giant tree bedecked with blazing orange flowers, while overhead a flock of blue-crowned motmot birds with matching indigo tail feathers swooped and soared. Small lizards striped with all the colors of a Crayola box skittered across every surface. Just a short distance from the main house, we discovered a friendly herd of goats.

"This place is awesome," Josephine gushed as we stopped to pet a young kid with fuzz-topped horns just beginning to push up.

Though I tried to counter her at every turn simply for the sake of it, I couldn't find much to grumble about. Rather than agree though, I simply deflected. "What do you think these green things are?"

Oblong with one end tapering down to a softly rounded point, multitudes of the unidentified flora hung from a squat, broad-topped tree at the edge of the pasture.

"How the hell should I know?"

Pulling one down, I rolled it from one hand to the other. The exterior was hard and unyielding, reminiscent of an unripe walnut.

"Maybe it's a nut," I hypothesized.

Jo grinned. "There's definitely at least one nut in front of me right now."

"Takes one to know one," I replied, wishing I had a better comeback.

A few minutes later, we ran into the inn's groundskeeper trimming tropical topiaries in the front yard.

"Afternoon," he offered without pausing from snipping. "You the new guests?"

"We just got here this morning," replied Jo. "We've been exploring."

"Maybe you can help us," I joined in as I pulled out my mystery find. "Do you know what this is?"

Clip clip went the shears. "Mango, not ripe enough to eat; you picked it too early."

"Is it good for anything?" I asked.

A shake of the head. "It's good for throwing away."

Jo chose to process this situation differently. "You just murdered a baby mango!" she screamed as only an enraged teenage girl can. "How could you?"

"You can't kill a piece of fruit." I looked over to the groundskeeper for backup, but he was clearly wishing he could fade into the foliage and refused to make eye contact. "That doesn't even make any sense."

"What doesn't make any sense is why you would slaughter an infant in cold blood without a second thought," Jo tearfully exploded, before turning on her heel and stomping off toward the pool.

Though Jo and I argued regularly, her meltdowns could usually be attributed to a very obvious point of contention. Getting freaked out over a piece of fruit didn't make any sense. I stood there for a second, not sure what the social protocol was when you've been accused of horticultural homicide.

"Sometimes she can be a little crazy," I explained to the groundskeeper, circling my pointer finger next to my right ear. "Sorry about that."

He gave me one of those awkward nods that implied he was pretty sure we were both a little loco, then turned back to his pruning project.

Josephine and I avoided each other for the next couple of hours until our parents returned from their foraging excursion. My father managed to single-handedly improve our collective spirits by bringing back a selection of locally made sweets, including sesame-covered balls bound together by molasses cores, shredded coconut patties, and dulce-de-leche-like coconut fudge that instantly became a lifelong obsession.

"You can enjoy some of it after lunch," my mother decreed. "We brought you some roti and Bentleys to drink."

The latter turned out to be a sweetly tart homemade lime soda with a not unappealing bite courtesy of a couple dashes of locally made

Angostura bitters. It was the perfect pairing for the spicy yellow curry covering the chunks of chicken inside the crepe-like roti wrapper.

As we ate, my father perused the guidebook. Knowing his fly-by-the-seat-of-his-pants style, I was pretty sure it was the first time he had opened it. I guessed this public display of reading was an effort to tame my mother's belief that he played our vacations a little too loosey-goosey for her taste.

"What beach do you want to hit tomorrow?" he queried. "It looks like we have some good options – Man of War Bay, Bloody Bay, Pirate's Bay."

"Sounds very relaxing, Ralph," my mother deadpanned. "What about a day by the pool instead?"

"We didn't come all this way to lounge," Dad rejoined. "We need to explore! Right, kids?"

Jo had no interest in being dragged into their conflict. "Whatever, Dad."

With a hint of uncharacteristic desperation, he turned to me with a keening, hopeful look in his eyes, like a dog that wanted to go outside for a spirited game of fetch. All Dad desired was one partially enthusiastic member of the family to validate his excitement and go along with whatever half-baked plan came to his mind. For the first time ever, I realized that I could choose to not be involved. I didn't have to be his accomplice.

Frankly, I was more interested in a day by the pool myself. The trio of ominously titled bays only sounded like an intriguing proposition if I could explore them by myself, preferably with a map for long-lost treasure in hand.

"The pool does sound nice," I offered hesitantly. "I could use a little R&R."

My father's face fell but only for a second. His look of disappointment was quickly replaced by a pout that managed to look stern. "We're doing something," he insisted. "We're not going to be doing nothing down by the pool."

He slammed the guidebook shut. "You all need to be a little more adventurous," he told us. "We're in paradise; embrace it."

* * * * *

In the early pre-dawn hours of the next morning, my father woke me up by loudly embracing paradise.

"God-fucking-dammit!" I heard him yell through the thin wall that divided our rooms. "What the fuck?"

I sat bolt upright, unsure of where I was or what was happening. It was still dark outside and a tempestuous storm raged. Rain beat against our window, zigzags of lightning crackled through the blackness, and I could hear tree branches wetly slapping against each other.

"What's he so damn upset about?" Jo asked sleepily from her bed on the other side of the room. "Is he still pissed we didn't want to go to the beach?"

"I have no idea," I muttered. "I almost don't want to find out."

I was curious about what could cause my father to freak out so loudly though, so I padded down the hall and hesitantly knocked on my parents' door. Mom answered in her nightgown, her eyes still not completely open.

Before I could inquire about the commotion, she simply said, "Your father forgot to close the window before we went to bed."

Opening the door all the way, I saw Dad dredging wet clothes and soaked camera equipment from the bowels of his super-sized suitcase. As he ferried them to the bathroom, he kept up a steady stream of obscenities – "Shit! Fuck! Goddamn it!" He was so intent in wringing out and hanging up his clothing and finding spots where his electronics could dry out that he didn't even acknowledge I was there.

"Just go back to bed," my mother urged. "There's nothing you can do. We'll see you in the morning."

I gave her a quick hug and beat a hasty retreat back to my own room.

"Dad didn't close the window," I explained to Jo. "All of his stuff is completely soaked."

"Classic," Jo murmured. "Let's hope his camera is waterlogged so he can't shoot his usual seven million rolls of film."

Unfortunately for us, I found out the next day that my father's expensive Nikon survived the monsoon.

"Get a little closer to the cannons," he urged me, motioning with his right hand while aiming the camera with his left. "They're not going to bite."

We came looking for the impressive-sounding Fort Cambleton overlooking Man of War Bay but quickly realized that despite the beautiful views, the stronghold's majesty had been overstated. What was purported to be one of the original fortresses that had protected the island from buccaneers, pirates, and a rotating cast of Europeans – depending on who claimed ownership of the island at the time – was instead nothing more than a pair of cannons that we later discovered were referred to by local historians as simply Cambleton Battery.

Annoyed and unappeased, Dad decided we should check out a nearby lighthouse that his guidebook recommended. According to a local we stopped to ask for directions, it was only "a little way away." After more than 20 minutes of maneuvering our rental car over a pothole-pocked dirt road along the northern shoreline, we finally discovered that the designation "lighthouse" was just as accurate as "fort."

A small scaffolding – maybe two stories high – stood between the roadway and the cliffs plunging down to the Caribbean Sea. At the top, a single light bulb perched forlornly. Since it was daylight, it wasn't even on.

"Seriously?" Jo muttered. "We came all the way out into the middle of nowhere for this?"

"It looks like it was built for gnomes," I offered, fruitlessly attempting to lighten the mood. Not even my father bothered pretending that he was going to get out. Instead, we all just sat there silently for a few moments, the car idling as radiant sunbeams pierced the windows like we were ants under a magnifying glass.

That evening, we had more success when we drove into a nearby town to watch the calypso semi-finals. The regional winner would go on to compete in the championships in Port of Spain over on Trinidad. The top-ranked acts there would earn highly prized headlining slots during the Carnival festivities.

A modest stage was set up in the town center, where a rotating cast of wannabe kings and queens of calypso showcased their steelpan-powered tunes. In front, a loud and opinionated crowd raucously voiced their diverging opinions of the acts. One faction would start a hearty cheer, only to be drowned out by boos from another quarter. That would inspire the cheering contingent to scream louder, which in turn inspired more boos.

Everyone seemed to be able to agree on only two things: the beer and the dancing. No matter where you looked, someone was slamming back a bottle of Carib lager and everyone danced whether they loved or hated the band. This was different from the dancing at the kava ceremony; it was energetic and exhibitionist. The hip shaking, pelvis thrusting, and mad gyrations were worthy of an MTV video. If I wasn't a stand-in-the-corner kid, they were the kind of moves I'd have liked to try out at the next high school dance.

When we joined the rambunctious, undulating mass, the group on stage sounded like a herd of cats being blended into a most unappetizing milkshake. The caterwauling lead singer was so out of sync with the band that it was almost as if they were giving two completely different concerts.

From my perspective, the only redeeming thing about this musical massacre was the trio of scantily clad women singing backup.

Beguilingly swaying their hips to the beat and thrusting their considerable chests out with every "yeah yeah yeah," they were unwittingly singing a siren's call to this hormonally charged 16-year-old virgin.

These vixen vocalists were definitely a far cry from the sanitized sensuality of the Bangles, who I'd seen in concert a year earlier. These island girls danced liked they felt it; Susanna Hoffs and company just did what they felt they were supposed to do. Gazing all too intently at the three belting babes, I discovered the true meaning of soul singing.

My father interrupted my minor epiphany with his best, completely unintentional impression of Speedy Gonzales.

"*¡Ándale! ¡Arriba! ¡Arriba!*" he brayed as he began demonstrating a set of dance moves that had peaked in popularity sometime in the early 1950s. "Come on, Alison, my *chica!*"

To her credit, my mother began cutting the rug with an ease that all three of her traveling companions found at least somewhat surprising. Jo shook her hair and wobbled her shoulders, a dance move that only really counts if you're a young woman. I did my best to move my body as little as possible while still creating the impression that I was dancing. Self-conscious doesn't begin to describe how I felt when I was in mixed-sex group social situations. The fact that I referred to them as "mixed-sex group social situations" tells you all you really need to know about my ability to be absurdly awkward.

When the calypso band brought their set to a fiery finish, it seemed like the response was unanimously positive. Not that I could hear very much myself – I was letting loose with an impressive wail that rivaled anything Meatloaf ever put down on tape.

"Calm down, dude," Jo yelled at me after my high-pitched hollering passed the minute marker. "These guys suck."

"But did you see those backup singers?" I gushed after I had run out of steam, eyes ablaze with teenage lust and half panting. "The Pips have nothing on them."

"I don't know about that," Mom, a longtime Motown fan, chastised. "The singer certainly couldn't compare to Gladys Knight."

Dad took our debate as a sign that we were all enjoying ourselves and used this moment to offer up his latest starry-eyed scheme.

"We should extend our vacation so we can go to Carnival," he enthused. "Just think – nothing but calypso from sunup to sundown."

It was easy to imagine such a fate, and it was hardly an appealing one. This was clearly a failed venture for all of us. My parents weren't getting along, and I wasn't getting along with either Josephine or my father. Why prolong this uncomfortable situation? This Old Yeller of a vacation needed to be taken out back and promptly shot. My mother and I were clearly on the same page because she moved to cut off this particular line of thinking.

"Ralph," she started with a velveteen tone that barely hid a steel backbone, "don't forget that we have to get the kids back to school."

Dad's face clouded over. "You're no fun," he sulked, before trying to act like he had the upper hand in the debate. "We'll talk about it more later."

"Mmm hmm," Mom hummed, blatantly uninterested in changing her opinion on this particular topic. "Maybe you'll be thinking clearly by then."

Dad didn't take her sharp salvo well. "Maybe you'll have found your sense of fun, Alison," he grumbled before turning his attention back to the stage where the next act looked ready to assault the crowd with their calypso craziness.

Jo and I found our first moment of solidarity on this trip as we exchanged a worried glance. Mom and Dad usually made it a point to not fight in front of us. It was starting to feel like Tobago was going to be ground zero for a marital meltdown.

146

The atmosphere failed to lighten during the next couple of days. If anything, the storm clouds darkened over my parents, who got progressively colder and quieter toward each other.

One morning we drove to Arnos Vale on the northwestern shore in hopes of having a mood-brightening lunch at its well-known oceanfront hotel.

"I'm so sorry, but we're booked up," the maître d' told us apologetically after quickly peering at the hefty reservations ledger that filled the podium in front of him.

My father wasn't willing to simply throw in the towel. "Are you sure you couldn't squeeze us in? We don't take up much space."

The maître d' shut his book with a definitive thump. "I wish I could, but the hotel is sold out right now. We need to save the tables for guests."

"With hospitality like this, I can see why they'd want to stay here," my father replied, doing nothing to hide his sarcasm.

"I'm sure there's somewhere else nice nearby," my mother interjected. "Can you recommend anything?" She gave the gatekeeper a wide smile that seemed to say, "Don't mind him. He gets cranky when he's hungry."

Turning to face my mother, the maître d' relented, "Of course. Pigeon Point is just down the road. There are some nice restaurants right on the beach."

"That sounds lovely. We really appreciate your help. Right, Ralph?"

His agreement sounded more like a disgruntled harrumph. "Let's get out of here, Alison."

"Thank you," my mother called over her shoulder as we filed back to the car in low spirits. Our mood momentarily lightened when we pulled up at our destination. Pigeon Point was a postcard-ready slice of the Caribbean. Turquoise waters lapped at a long curving stretch of golden sand edged by arching palm trees, which provided beachgoers with the option of refreshing shade on this scorching day.

Jo and I had our seatbelts unbuckled and had gotten out before my father had even turned off the car. I wanted to do nothing more than put on my snorkeling gear and dive into the ocean, but Dad quickly squelched that plan. "We're getting a bite to eat first," he mandated. "Then you can go in."

With a few rolls of the eyes, we dutifully followed him and Mom over to a small restaurant overlooking the beach. In the shade of the thatched roof, the sandy concrete floor stayed cool, while a nice breeze blew in from the sea. White plastic tables and matching chairs were scattered across the space. There was a small gift shop attached to the bar area in the back of the room.

"Can we pick up some postcards first?" Jo asked. "I want to send some to my friends."

"Don't you mean your boyfriends?" I asked as annoyingly as possible.

"Shut up, Nevin," she shot back. "We all know that if you buy any postcards they won't be for your girlfriend – unless you want to send one to an imaginary person."

"All right, all right," Dad conceded in hopes of heading off an argument. "Let's see what they have."

The cramped boutique turned out to be packed to the gills with all manner of touristy tchotchkes. The shelves sported faded snow globes filled with antithetically tropical scenes, dusty polished shells, and shot glasses decorated with Trinidad and Tobago's flag. After picking up a few postcards featuring several of the local forts that we hadn't been able to find, I stopped at a clothes rack filled with bright neon T-shirts gussied up with steel drums and elaborately costumed Carnival dancers. I pulled off a medium in poison green, thinking it would pop against my black-and-white skater shorts.

I carried it over to my father, who was halfheartedly examining a laminated card of the local flora and fauna. "Can I get this, Dad?"

"I want one, too," Jo piped up from behind me.

He looked up from his reading. "Are you sure you're going to wear them?"

I didn't hesitate, even though I wasn't sure how this loud Tobagan gear would go over back in Clinton. "Of course, Dad."

"All right, give them to me."

He handed them to the young woman working at the counter.

"Are you enjoying your time on Tobago?" she asked while taking the shirts off their hangers and punching the prices into her ancient register.

"It's been interesting," Dad allowed as he reached into his pocket for his wallet. "Definitely full of surprises."

I couldn't tell if his irritation was due to low blood sugar or his general feelings about our vacation. I wasn't about to play psychologist to find out.

"I'm glad to hear it," said the clerk, mistaking his comments for positive praise. Then she added another surprise to his travel itinerary. "That will be 85 dollars, please."

My father's head snapped up so swiftly and sharply that I thought it was going to pop right off.

"Excuse me?" he asked, clearly not believing what he had heard. "Did you say 85 dollars? All we have are two T-shirts and some postcards."

The clerk lifted the price tags on the hangers. "The T-shirts are 37.50 each, sir."

Jo and I began edging backward, not wanting the blame for this

149

eruption. Not looking where I was going, I bumped into my mother, who was also keeping herself out of the fray.

"Who the hell pays almost 40 dollars for a T-shirt?" my father railed, though I wasn't sure if he was addressing the clerk, us, or maybe God. "I could buy a nice dinner for all of us for what you're charging. Forget it."

Leaving the merchandise on the counter, he walked toward us and – for some reason I still can't explain – I felt the need to ask for an unnecessary clarification.

"Does this mean we're not getting the postcards either?"

For a second, he looked as if he would transform into a giant werewolf and devour me on the spot. I shrank before my father wondering why on earth I had opened my big fat mouth. If those were going to be my last words, I wished I had said something more meaningful than an inquiry about a postcard purchase.

Luckily, he pulled himself together. "Everyone get in the car," he ordered as he moved toward the door. "We're getting out of here."

My mother decided to weigh in with her own line of questioning. "Aren't you hungry still?"

He didn't stop. "I've lost my appetite."

* * * * *

In an attempt to defibrillate our dying vacation, a group outing was planned to Little Tobago. The uninhabited island was lavishly praised in Dad's guidebook as a miniature Eden rife with rare birds and exotic wildlife.

"Are we going to see any giant tortoises?" Jo wondered aloud as the motorboat carried us from Speyside on the northern tip of Tobago to the lush isle just 20 minutes away.

"You're going to be blown away by all the animals," my father assured her as he checked over his photography gear and loaded up

150

the bandolier on his camera bag with nearly a dozen extra rolls of Kodak. "I just hope I brought enough film."

Disembarking on a small dock, we walked toward the jungle where a rough path wound its way deeper into the vegetation. There were no markers or a conveniently placed map to indicate what we were getting into.

"The tours here are self-guided," Dad remarked as he charged ahead with his camera at the ready.

"Do you know where you're going?" I asked as we all fell in single file behind him.

"You can't get lost on an island this small," Dad declared as he stalked forward with his head tilted upward on the hunt for portraiture candidates.

That line of reasoning didn't make any sense to me, but looking behind us, I could just make out the small motorboat that had brought us beginning to trace its route homeward. It was set to return for us in a few hours, so I offered a silent prayer that the captain wouldn't forget us. It wasn't my habit to disobey my father since I valued the regular dispersal of my allowance and didn't like being grounded on the weekends. Turning around and marching forward, I dutifully followed him into the unknown.

After walking through dense tropical woodland for several minutes, we came to a small clearing. At the center was a dilapidated hut with peeling paint, a roof pockmarked with holes, and broken shutters by the windows. The newest element was a pristine placard nailed next to the sagging front door that read "Maintained by the government of Trinidad and Tobago."

"Does 'maintained' mean something else in the Caribbean?" I joked, but no one chuckled.

My father was examining several hand-painted wooden signs, which pointed to a number of pathways leading even deeper into the foliage.

151

"Yellowtail Trail sounds promising," he said as he began walking onward without further consultation.

Lacking any other options, we all trudged behind him up the gently rising slope of the forest floor. I could hear birds twittering in the treetops, but I couldn't spot them in the dense canopy. Every time I heard a distinct chirp, cheep, or warble, I would stop and stare intently at the area that I would have sworn was the source of the sound. Since Jo was nipping at my heels – probably to ensure that she wouldn't lose us, her only means off this godforsaken speck – she would stumble into me. As deterrence, she began walking with her fists balled up and her arms crooked, like she was competing in a live version of Rock 'Em, Sock 'Em Robots.

Suddenly there was a tweet from just over my head. I halted abruptly and was rewarded with a pair of punches to my midsection.

"Move it, idiot," Jo raged.

I held her off with one arm while craning my head back. I could hear birdsong so clearly above me, but there wasn't a single life form – winged or otherwise – to be seen. There were these odd structures hanging from the limbs though. They looked like hairy testicles.

"Are those Paul Bunyan's balls?" I wondered aloud.

"Do you want a punch in your balls?" Jo replied. "Stop moving again and you'll get one."

There was an energetic flipping of the guidebook's pages from the front of our backwoods conga line. "I believe those are yellowtail nests," my father proclaimed. "We must be at the heart of their territory. Keep your eyes peeled. We're bound to see them any second now."

We charged forward searching the foliage with renewed hope. I examined every branch, nest, and vine in the hopes that it might be concealing one of the much-vaunted yellowtails. Their calls were ringing through the forest more loudly now, as if taunting us. Each tweet was a further insult, a small slap across our faces for our incompetency.

Despite Dad's optimism, seconds turned into minutes, which turned into what seemed like decades. Every step was more boring than the last. This was no miniature Eden. This whopping disappointment was certainly nothing to boast about when we got back to Clinton – unless I wanted to tell my classmates how we went on the dullest and most birdless bird watching expedition of all time. Not exactly the stuff of legends.

I felt like I could use a few legends to bolster my image back home. If I wanted to go to college, I had to get through the gauntlet of high school. That didn't necessarily mean socially thriving but – at the very least – surviving. A few stories about how I had lived through some crazy adventures in the Caribbean would add a missing edge of bad-assery and a few myth-building battle scars to my generally well-polished and well-behaved reputation. The Yellowtail Trail was not yielding the types of Indiana Jones-style escapades I desired.

Suddenly, there was exaggerated shushing from the front of the line as my father came to an abrupt halt. He gestured frantically to the three of us to join him. We all crowded behind him, peering forward to see what had caused this unexpected stop. Had we finally discovered the elusive yellowtail?

Dad pointed in front of us about 30 feet away. For a second, I didn't see anything more exciting than a cluster of princess-pink hibiscus flowers. Big whoop. Nothing to get excited about.

Then I saw the reason for his excitement hovering in the air – a lone hummingbird. It wasn't even a particularly exciting hummingbird. In fact, it was a very average-looking one – the kind that we had seen dozens of times both in the States and abroad.

Usually a hummingbird was only worthy of a casual comment and maybe a few moments of half-interested observation. Today, this unremarkable specimen was absolutely transfixing.

We all gazed at it like it was something truly fantastical – a white tiger, a unicorn, or the Loch Ness Monster. Over the hum of the jungle I could just make out the low rapid-fire click of my father's camera as he endlessly documented this not-so-historic moment.

This was ridiculous. I wanted to briskly slap everyone, shake their shoulders like I was Lennie playing with the rabbits, and scream, "It's a fricking hummingbird, people! Let's move on with our lives!"

Everyone seemed too on edge for this tactic to go over well. I didn't want to be the straw that broke this camel's back. So I simply stood still in the middle of the jungle not saying a word. I kept all my frustration with the failure of this expedition tightly coiled inside me. My eyes zoned out as I stared at the bird – its head and body in focus, the wings a flickering blur. It weaved in between the hibiscus, pausing now and then for a quick sip.

The camera clicks stopped, and the film began to noisily rewind. The sudden change in sounds startled the star of the only one-man show in town. The hummingbird turned toward us for a microsecond before zipping off in the opposite direction.

We were all quiet for a long moment, and then my father broke the silence. "Well, that was..."

"A hummingbird," Jo finished with all the enthusiasm of a customer service rep on the late shift.

As he popped in a fresh canister of Kodak, my father still refused to curtail his misplaced enthusiasm for this jaunt through the jungle.

"That was just the beginning," he vowed. "The yellowtails are just around the next bend."

Turning back around to lead his dispirited band, he restarted our jinxed journey down the path. Approaching the turn, he anticipatorily brought his camera to his eye and stealthily stalked forward. He disappeared around the corner, and I strained to hear the click of the camera. There was a moment of silence, then a human explosion.

"You've got to be fucking kidding me!" I heard him roar, startling me so much that I recoiled backward into my sister, who took the opportunity to punch me twice in the side.

My mother ran ahead, clearly alarmed. "What's wrong?"

Not wanting to be left out, Josephine and I followed her around the bend. We almost ran smack dab into my parents, who were standing in front of a large tree where the trail came to an abrupt dead end.

"This is bullshit," my father raged. "Who builds a trail that goes nowhere? You wouldn't see this kind of shoddy workmanship at Yosemite."

No matter what the situation, my mother insisted on maintaining decorum. "Language, Ralph."

"I can't believe we came all this way for nothing," he fumed. "I'm going to write the publishers of the guidebook and demand my money back."

That sounded like a good way for him to amuse himself when we got back to Clinton, but the real question was what were we going to do now?

"Do you want to backtrack and try one of the other trails?" my mother tentatively offered with a complete lack of enthusiasm. "We might find something there."

"The only thing I want to find is a glass of scotch and a comfortable chair on the deck back at the Richmond Great House," my father huffed. "Let's get the hell out of here."

* * * * *

The next day, I was sitting by the pool with my diary in hand. The cook had hooked me up with a glass of orange juice and some cookies, and the weather was beautiful, so I had no complaints. Mom was up in her room taking a nap, Jo was off somewhere, and Dad was at one of the nearby ports to see if he could arrange for a fishing expedition.

Alone time on a family vacation was extremely rare, and a moment like this was to be prized. I took a sip of OJ, nibbled on a crunchy sugar cookie, and pondered the best way to mock our failed ornithological expedition. Should I call the Yellowtail Trail a hoax or a swindle? And were we bamboozled, hornswoggled, or simply deceived?

"What are you doing?" My sister's peevish voice cut through my thesaurus debate. So much for my solo sojourn.

I closed my diary and turned to stare her down. "I was trying to do some writing, but it doesn't look like that's going to happen now."

She didn't care what I had been doing because she had clearly come down to take a dip. Dropping her towel on the chair beside mine, she daintily walked down the steps into the water and began carefully sculling across the pool without letting her hair get wet. Pausing at the side, she splashed water at me.

"Afraid of a little water, wimp?" she jeered.

"No. Are you afraid of becoming the most annoying person ever? Oh wait, never mind. You already are that person."

"Bite me," she shot back, along with a hearty flick of water that came close to dousing my diary. That wouldn't do. It was time to teach her a lesson. And pay her back for all her punches on the Yellowtail Trail.

I took off my shirt. "You know what? I could use a little a time in the water."

Running to the edge, I leapt into the air, pulled my legs in, grabbed my shins, squeezed my eyes shut, and bowed my head. The splash sounded like a clap of thunder. When I resurfaced, Jo was dripping wet with a look of pure murder in her eyes.

"You're a dick!" she screamed. "I hate you."

I smiled. "That's what you get for bothering me."

"Well, this is what you get for bothering me," she shouted as she reached to the side of the water where a long pool strainer was sitting. Picking it up with both hands like it was broadsword, she swung it at me with all her enraged might. Everything happened so quickly that I barely had time to try to dive out of its way.

My reflexes weren't quick enough. She struck me with a glancing blow just above my right eye. I fell with a graceless splash, yelping in pain. Water rushed into my mouth as I plunged below the surface. I shot back up to the open air coughing hoarsely. Standing up unevenly, I held one hand in front of me to ward off another blow as I brought my other hand to my forehead. My fingers came away streaked with red, even as a throbbing pain began mingling with the stinging of chlorine on an open wound.

"Goddamn it," I turned and half-swam, half-ran to the shallow end, where I assumed Jo was still standing. The strainer was floating in the water, its edge tinted with a dash of crimson, but my sister was already out of the pool and well on her way back to the house.

"You'd better run," I yelled after her. "You're going to pay for this."

I got out of the pool, dried off, and sat down on a bamboo bench in the shade. My head ached, but there was a nice breeze, plenty of sunshine, and a few remaining cookies to help boost my spirits. I didn't understand why Jo was in such a combative mood lately. Though we had usually bickered, our arguments on this trip were more intense than ever before.

Rather than trying to unravel this mystery, I started reading my latest assignment for English class – *Lord of the Flies*. It turned out to be quite disconcerting given my current circumstances. Reading the story of being marooned on a tropical island with a control freak named Ralph cut a little too close. The image of Ralph running away from a storm of spears was slightly more uplifting, though I didn't have any such weaponry on hand.

As I was weighing whether I should restart working on my diary entry or go inside the house in search of an alternate amusement,

Josephine reappeared. She was loping across the lawn on an angle toward the pool but on a trajectory that would keep a buffer zone of about 50 feet between us.

"Come back to get your bludgeon?" I asked, my voice drenched in equal parts sarcasm and bile. "Or to apologize?"

"Neither," she spat. "I'm here to tell you that you're no longer my brother."

This was a new spin to a long-running rivalry. Looking for a bad-ass response, I pulled out a retort that I'd heard my grandmother use on occasion. "Good riddance to bad rubbish."

"Whatever, dude." Jo kept walking until she had disappeared into the jungle on the far side of the pool.

Sitting back down on the bench with a satisfied air, I nonchalantly cracked open my journal and began funneling my frustration with Jo onto the page.

A few minutes later, I was deeply involved in crafting a particularly vitriolic passage about why I hated her when there was a clatter on the concrete to my left.

What the hell?

There was another sharp clicking of two hard surfaces colliding, then a small splash.

Was it another hailstorm of coconuts like in Fiji? Death by coconut was still near the bottom of my list of ways I wanted to die. Holding my hand over my head, I looked up and spotted my sister peeking out from behind a tree trunk at the far side of the pool.

She had a rock in her left hand cocked behind her shoulder. With what little might she had at her disposal, she hurled it at me, but it fell short and wide. Undeterred, she threw another one, which only traveled half the distance between us.

"Nice try," I taunted with a chuckle as yet another missile failed to come anywhere close.

Searching the nearby ground, I found a few stones and began returning fire. Unfortunately, my marksmanship had not improved since the Azores. The closest I got to hitting her was when one of my shots bounced off a branch above her and ricocheted in her general direction.

"No wonder you don't play baseball," Jo mocked.

"Whatever. You'd get picked last in gym class for a Wiffle ball team."

"At least I can do a pull-up."

She hit a nerve with her last barb, but my aim was so bad I couldn't deliver a forceful response. The best I could do was show her how little I feared her, so I gathered up my stuff and headed inside where I documented the whole incident in my diary.

As I was writing, I began to really think through why we were quarrelling so frequently and so viciously. If my friends with younger brothers and sisters were to be believed, some of this could be chalked up to normal sibling rivalries at this age.

That couldn't be all of it though. I felt unsettled by my parents' constant fighting; no doubt Jo was equally disturbed. Hopefully, their distress was temporary, a passing phase, a pothole in the road. Despite my moments of conflict with my family, I couldn't imagine a world without us in it together.

Things were still strained when we all piled in the rental car the next morning to spend a few hours at a nearby beach. The 15-minute ride seemed to last forever. The friction between Josephine and I precluded any conversation in the backseat, and the mood seemed equally frosty in the front. Not even the calypso tunes blaring out of the staticky radio helped.

Thankfully, the sandy sliver of beach was completely deserted and offered us just enough space to separate ourselves. Laying my towel down in the shade, I headed into the ocean. I swam out past where the waves were crashing into frothy explosions. I'd tread water until a sizable breaker began rolling in, paddle fast to gain momentum, and then use myself as a human boogie board to ride it toward the shore. Sometimes I'd mistime my body surfing and the waves would pull me under, tumble me about like a baseball in a blender, and then spit me back up with stinging eyes and a mouth full of brine.

I didn't care. Out here, I was free from everyone and everything. There was no high school dating drama, sibling rivalry, or parental issues. Just me and the sea. Too bad I couldn't stay out here in the water forever. If only there were a little island with room service and a library where I could pass the days in solitude.

After almost an hour, I caught the perfect wave and let it carry me into the shallows. Standing up, I took stock of the activity on the beach. Mom was reading in the shade while Jo appeared to be looking for shells at the high-tide line. And what was Dad doing? Seriously, what the hell was he doing?

He had stripped off every stitch of clothing and was strolling down the beach completely naked. The family jewels – framed by a pale white loincloth of untanned skin – dangled in the sea breeze. He had found a bag somewhere and was picking up garbage, making him look like a crazy custodian at a tropical nudist colony.

When we had lived in the farthest reaches of western New York, skinny-dipping had been one of Dad's favorite hobbies. However, there we lived on a secluded 200-acre property with four private ponds. The nearest neighbor was over a mile away, and we often went days without anyone other than the mailman driving by. At that time, my sister and I were little kids unaware of the social mores that now defined our lives as teenagers.

Spotting me emerging from the surf, my father headed my way. "Want to give me a hand, Nevin?" he hailed me in all his dubious glory.

I concentrated all of my attention on an imaginary point in the air just above his left shoulder and did my best not to blush. "Can I give you a fig leaf instead?"

He was unamused. "Stop being such a prude. You're worse than your mother."

"I'm not in the mood." I started walking toward the relative sanctuary of my towel. "I prefer to spend my vacations reading books – not picking up trash."

"You need to learn how to have fun," he warned me. "Someday you'll look back and wonder why you took life so seriously."

Dad's basic belief was that whatever he was doing was the epitome of fun. Anyone not interested in following his lead was automatically a party pooper.

"Sure. Whatever, Dad."

He continued his in-the-buff beach walk as I dried myself off.

Jo wandered over, yesterday's confrontation momentarily forgotten in light of Dad's au naturel stroll.

"Is he crazy?" she wondered aloud.

"Probably. What if someone comes down here?"

She giggled. "Oh my god, that would be so embarrassing. Can we pretend we don't know him?"

"We can certainly try."

Still laughing, Jo continued ambling down the beach toward where the car was parked and my father was bending over obscenely to gather a cluster of empty Carib cans. I picked up *Lord of the Flies* – determined to finish the assignment before the vacation was over so I didn't have to stay up all night the day before school – and had just started feeling sorry for Piggy when a shrill shriek shattered my concentration.

Looking up, I first saw my sister doing an able impression of Edvard Munch's "The Scream." Then I spotted what had caused her to squeal in embarrassed alarm: Two men paused on the steps

161

down to the beach about a dozen feet away. They had stopped because they had seen my birthday-suited father. Though they were frozen in place, Dad stayed in motion.

Dropping his trash bag, he walked toward them. Calmly scooping up his package with his left hand, he extended his right.

"Hello, I'm Robinson Crusoe."

You could have heard a fig leaf drop.

Neither of the newcomers made a move to become his Man Friday by shaking the proffered hand, though they couldn't stop staring at it. If they weren't wondering about the proper social response for this particularly peculiar situation, they were, at the very least, wondering where his hand had been given where the other one was currently positioned.

Josephine took this opportunity to scamper for the cover of the jungle underbrush, while I tucked myself behind the trunk of a nearby palm tree. As I peeked around the side, I wished that I had my father's camera. Finally, there was a moment on this trip to document, but who would believe me that something this bizarre had happened without tangible photographic proof?

While I was considering whether to dash over to the camera bag my father had left next to his now much-needed clothing, my mother exhibited her usual grace and quick thinking.

"He's not half as mad as he seems," she cheerily shouted as she hustled toward the standoff. "He's actually quite harmless."

Seeing a well-spoken woman in full dress seemed to reassure the visitors, who greeted her with all due civility.

"Good afternoon, is this a European beach?" the one on the left asked, intently looking in the opposite direction of my father and his clutched genitalia.

Mom gave a disarming chuckle. "My husband didn't think that anyone else would be coming down here."

162

"I was working on my tan," my father interjected, but everyone ignored him.

Jo appeared in the shrubbery beside me, clutching her stomach because she was still laughing so hard.

"Classic Dad," she managed to squeak out.

"Definitely. What the hell was he thinking?"

"No clue."

I shook my head. "I bet Mom is regretting that she married him right now."

* * * * *

Two days later, as Josephine and I were packing our bags before heading to the airport, there was a knock on the door and our parents walked in.

"There's been a slight change of plans," my mother began, a crestfallen look splashed across her face. "Your father is going to stay an extra week."

"I want to photograph the Carnival over on Trinidad," he added. "It's too unique an opportunity to pass up."

This turn of events was highly unusual. We always traveled as a quartet, even when I was wracked with tonsillitis in Western Samoa. Obviously, my father had realized that he couldn't have the kind of trip he wanted with us in tow.

"So you're abandoning us?" Jo asked, sounding more like a confused little girl than a blustery teen.

Dad moved to give her a hug, but she flinched away. "Never," he said, settling for a pat on her shoulders. "I'll be home before you know it. You'll take care of your mother and your sister, won't you, Nevin?"

I wasn't exactly sure what was being asked of me, but I agreed anyway. "Sure, Dad. I hope you get more pictures at Carnival than you did on the Yellowtail Trail."

Everyone smiled, but no one was in the mood to laugh. "That won't be difficult," he admitted. "Now finish packing; the taxi will be here in a little while."

Half an hour later, we were bidding Dad a final goodbye outside the Richmond Great House. The three of us were melancholic as we gave him hugs and asked him to be safe at Carnival. Getting into the backseat, we rolled down the windows and waved at him as the car proceeded down the driveway.

"Goodbye, Robinson Crusoe," I yelled out the window, but he didn't seem to hear me.

I slumped back into my seat, uninterested in talking or even reading. My mother and sister were equally subdued, so we let the stereo fill the void. The driver was playing Tracy Chapman, one of my mother's favorites. Heartfelt and filled with hurt, the songs were an all-too-perfect soundtrack. We were almost to the airport when my mother broke our silence by adding her voice to Chapman's with surprising strength.

I thought back to the four of us walking down the road under the stars in Savai'i, all of us singing "This Old Man." It seemed liked forever ago. Now our family was fractured, which shattered the seemingly unbreakable confidence that had manifested back in that moment. It felt like we were each on our own, islands adrift on a stormy sea in the pitch black of night. As I stared out the window of the cab, I wondered where we might be heading next.

Piranhas Don't Drink Scotch

[Venezuela & Colombia 1992, Age 17]

"Can anyone tell me where Venezuela is?" Our teacher looked at us like it was the toughest question in the world. Half the class put their hands up, including me.

Mr. Connelly's global studies class was one of my favorites because we got to study a lot of the places I'd traveled to. I could provide firsthand insights into New Zealand's Maori culture, talk with ease about rites of manhood in the South Pacific, and enlighten classmates about Caribbean food traditions. It was an easy A and I could be a showoff, which was a win-win for an honor roll dork like me.

Once a week, Mr. Connelly would do a rundown of major world events. It was a thankless attempt to distract us from the main reasons why his students read newspapers: the funny pages and sports scores. To keep all of us engaged for the duration, he turned these newscasts into Q&A sessions.

Mr. Connelly let a few of the football team's dimmer simians guess about Venezuela's location – Europe? To the left on the map? Next to Mexico? – before letting our future valedictorian answer.

"South America." My bespectacled classmate's response was an answer, not a question.

"Right, good. So this story takes place down in South America. There this guy Hugo" – he pronounced it like hugh-go, even though the lady on NPR always said ooh-go – "Chavez who tried to overthrow the government."

He began reading an article from *USA Today*, which I tuned out except for the headlines – dozens of casualties, thousands detained, ringleader arrested, government crackdown.

All this mayhem had flitted out of my thoughts by the time I sat down for dinner that night.

"A moment of silence, please," my mother asked us as she took my left hand and I reached over to grab Jo's. My sister gave me one of those "only 'cause Mom's making me" looks, but she took my outstretched palm.

We all bowed our heads obediently, and I stared down at the soft cotton napkin in my lap. The smell of my mom's ragù was so distracting that the thought of prayer instantly vanished. After a few moments, my mother squeezed my hand. "Thank you."

I was never sure if she was thanking us for humoring her or whether she was offering up an appreciation to the divine.

"Jo, take some salad. Nevin, would you like a slice of bread?"

Grabbing the pasta tongs, my father heaped a tangle of spaghetti onto a plate. "Alison, do you want to tell them or should I?"

"Go ahead."

He smiled like a kid who just got permission to open two presents on Christmas Eve. "We're going on a trip."

Really? This could be fun. Or it could be a shit-show. It was always a coin toss with Dad in charge.

Jo piped up. "Where?"

"Los Roques," he said grandly, as if it was the name of an opulent palace that people spent their whole lives dreaming of visiting.

My Spanish wasn't great, but I was pretty sure that meant The Rocks. That didn't sound too promising. "We're going to The Rocks?" I asked.

"They're islands," Dad explained as he passed down my plate full of spaghetti. "*National Geographic* said that they're like the Galapagos but more remote and pristine."

166

My first thought was, "Let's hope they are a step up from Mini Tobago and the Yellowtail Trail," but I kept my mouth shut.

Jo clearly didn't remember our encounter with a lone hummingbird because her imagination was running wild. "Are there giant iguanas? Tortoises? Sea lions?"

"I'm sure there are," said my father in a far-too-easygoing tone of voice, which probably meant he had no idea what he was talking about. "The whole island and the ocean around it are a nature preserve."

Not wanting to be negative – and still holding out hope that there might be something of interest, like the giant head statues of Easter Island – I decided to take an optimistic approach to this latest trip. "That sounds like it could be cool," I said. "What are we going to be doing out there?"

As soon as the question left my mouth, I knew the answer. What else do you do on an island that would inspire my father to fly into the unknown?

"A lot of deep-sea fishing," Dad replied predictably. "It *is* in the middle of the ocean." He smiled at his own joke.

"There's a ton of other stuff, too," Mom added. "Nevin, the butter, please."

"The beach, snorkeling, hiking in the nature preserve," my father ticked off these activities with a pointed thrust of the ladle he'd be using for the marinara.

I had only one more question. "Where exactly is it, Dad?"

He looked up from twirling a forkful of spaghetti into a messy ball. "It's actually part of Venezuela."

I flashed back to class.

Dozens of casualties. Thousands detained. Ringleader arrested. Government crackdown.

Shit.

* * * * *

I hesitantly stepped out of the plane and climbed down the rickety staircase that extended to the cracked tarmac of Los Roques Airport. I wanted to scan beyond the runway to check for revolutionaries, but the bright glare of the sun hurt my eyes so much that I had them scrunched nearly closed. Through my eyelashes I could see only a few feet in front of me, so I kept my gaze locked on my mother's retreating purple flip-flops. If she started to run, I would follow her lead.

I checked in with my other senses for any evidence of nearby enemies. The blistering heat was a welcome change from the blustery cold of upstate New York, but it didn't tip me off to any guerilla snipers perched on top of the airport terminal. I could hear my father thanking the cabin staff behind me and the whine of another plane's engines revving up nearby, but there were no sounds of machine gunfire, the explosions of mortar rounds, or the cries of an oncoming horde of revolutionaries.

I let out a sigh of relief and took a deep breath. What the fuck? A suffocating mélange of eau de dump fire and parfum de trash filled my nostrils and instantaneously turned my stomach into a roiling maelstrom threatening to bring up the reheated mess billed as chicken cordon bleu served on the La Guardia-to-Caracas leg of our trip.

"What the hell is that smell?" I heard my father exclaim somewhere behind me.

Unwilling to open my mouth to answer, I held my breath and picked up my pace. Thankfully, the terminal was just a few feet away.

Cooler and dimmer, it reeked of industrial-strength cleaning agents. Normally I would have wrinkled my nose in disgust, but for once the acrid chemical scents were a welcome alternative. I took the break from the afternoon sun to dig my Black Crowes baseball cap out of my backpack and pull it down low over my eyes.

Way to go, Dad. Galapagos, my ass.

My mother and father stepped to the side to confer about something, so Josephine began noncommittally flipping through an issue of *Seventeen* that my father had bought without consulting her first.

"*Highlights* would have been a better choice," she fumed. "Can I borrow your *Rolling Stone?*"

"Maybe when I'm done with it."

"Bastard."

I opened my magazine to the photo spread featuring the cast of *90210*. "Do you think I'm more Brenda's type or Kelly's?"

Jo glared at me. "You don't have a chance with either of them, dick."

My father interrupted our little tête-à-tête with a bark. "Get your stuff together."

I shouldered my navy backpack and stuffed the magazine into its front pocket. My parents led us to the tiny baggage area, which was basically a hole in the wall between the runway and the terminal. Through the dirty plastic curtain that covered the gap, I could see a porter wearing aviator sunglasses, giant black earmuffs, and an oil-stained tan jumpsuit unloading our luggage. His movements were very leisurely until it came time to deliver the bags, which he did by hurling them through the flap and onto the floor of the terminal. Mom's hot pink Fiorucci bag with black polka dots landed with a thump just a few feet away from us.

"Hey, watch what you're doing," my father yelled through the gap, but the porter just gestured at his earmuffs and smiled broadly before chucking what turned out to be Dad's black Samsonite at his feet.

"Some hospitality," he muttered as he picked it up. "I thought Venezuelans were supposed to be friendly." He clearly hadn't been reading *The New York Times* he buried himself in during breakfast each morning.

With our bags in tow, we headed back outside to the taxi stand. I imagined we would be on the edge of a pristine jungle crawling with exotic fauna. Unfortunately, the Amazonian wonderland of my dreams was nothing more than a parking lot dotted with litter. Sun-bleached Doritos bags, empty Coke bottles, and endless pages of newspaper blew across the concrete stretch. And the stink was back. God, what was that smell?

My father wasn't amused by this ugly reality. He stood there in the mid-afternoon heat instantly sweating through the jeans and sweater he had put on that morning in snowy upstate New York.

"This isn't at all like the pictures in the magazine," he fumed. "I'm going to write a letter to the editor."

"Let's see what the rest of the island is like before we jump to conclusions," Mom said as we plodded over to the first taxi in line. "This could just be the bad part of town or something."

My optimism was fading quickly, but I wasn't about to get in between my parents on this one. This vacation was already a first-class fiasco, and I didn't want to exacerbate the situation.

Unfortunately, the ride to our hotel didn't raise my expectations. The wind rushing in the windows obliterated some of the smells, but it couldn't excise the underlying stench that was apparently the island's olfactory calling card. It was like a sewage plant on fire. This must be what they meant when they coined the term "shithole." What an awful place to be gunned down by strangers.

The scenery flashing by was unsettling for someone expecting vistas worthy of Darwin's journal. Though I had seen photos of pristine beaches and quaint Caribbean one-story dwellings, none of them were in evidence. There were rundown shacks that passed for homes, while the one sandy stretch we passed featured a colorful cornucopia of trash scattered across it. My father sat in the passenger seat growing increasingly quiet but more visibly perturbed, as if each new scene were slapping him across the face.

170

In the backseat, my mother perched between my sister and me, a hand on each of our legs. She didn't need to worry about us fighting. Both Josephine and I were clearly shell-shocked by what had been billed as a vacation destination but looked more like a post-nuclear wasteland. This would be a perfect location to shoot *Mad Max 4: So Fucking Far Beyond Thunderdome You Wouldn't Believe Me If I Told You*.

The taxi came to a halt in front of a ramshackle two-story house that looked like it was caving in on itself. Its walls were leaning inward at an angle and the windows sliding off like something from a Dali painting. The front door bulged outward from the frame like a buckle on a too-tight belt.

When I turned back to look at Dad, his face had become a bright shade of killer tomato red.

"What the hell is this?"

"The hotel," the cab driver replied with a shrug.

"Bullshit."

We didn't even get out.

Just a few hours later, we found ourselves back on the mainland in the Caracas airport for the second time that day. While my mother, sister, and I slumped on our luggage in a passenger waiting area, my father ducked into a bar where he befriended a lapsed Venezuelan Mormon over a couple Cuba Libres.

I have Bacardi *con Coca Cola y limon* to thank for what happened next. By the bottom of the second glass, my father's new friend had convinced him we needed to fly to Puerto Ayacucho, a pinprick-on-a-map port town at the mouth of the Orinoco River. Without consulting the rest of us or soliciting a second opinion – perhaps from a passing Brazilian Episcopalian – my father bade farewell to his new *amigo* and got us seats on the next flight to Nowheresville, Venezuela.

"It's supposed to be beautiful," he told us with unchecked

excitement as he waved the already-purchased tickets in front of us like they were million-dollar bills. "Manuel – or was it Ricardo? – said it's the most beautiful place he's ever seen."

My mother frantically rifled through her guidebook in an attempt to locate Puerto Ayacucho, but it didn't seem to warrant its own section – never a good sign when you prize access to hospitals, embassies, and potable drinking water.

"This is going to be a real adventure," my father continued, undaunted by a silence punctuated only by the mad flipping of pages. "I hope you kids are ready for it."

I looked over at my sister. Fourteen going on 30, she looked as thrilled as only teenage girls can. Refusing to glance up from the book she was reading, Jo drawled, "Sounds *won-der-ful*, Dad, really *mar-vel-ous*. Have they discovered electricity yet?"

"You're going to love it," my father replied blithely. "Just wait and see."

We only had to wait an hour longer – after a short flight over nothing but uncivilized jungle that didn't look like it concealed any of the conveniences of modern living – to see what we were supposedly going to love. Frankly, Puerto Ayacucho's Cacique Aramare Airport looked like a rundown version of the airport we had left in upstate New York, just a little dirtier and a lot louder and the signs were in Spanish. Not exactly the kind of place that inspires swooning, though there was some cause for rejoicing.

"Look, Jo, light bulbs!" I pointed with exaggerated enthusiasm as we picked up our luggage and headed outside to find a ride into town and a hotel.

"Great," she deadpanned. "What are the chances they have working toilets?"

"I don't know, but at least this place doesn't smell like one."

Outside the terminal, a colorful cast of hustlers, charlatans, and veteran gold diggers flocked to us with pigeon cries of "Hello, my friend!" and "I take your luggage?" It was from this unheavenly host that one man distinguished himself. His slicked-back raven hair, denim shirt, and gold chain with a shark tooth hanging around his neck screamed swindler, but he spoke my father's language. "I give you a free ride to the besty hotel around, *mi amigos!*"

After spending a lot of money on what had thus far been a doomed vacation, the word "free" struck a chord with my father.

"I'm Ralph," he said and extended his hand, as if to both introduce himself and seal the deal on that free ride.

"I'm Rafael," proclaimed our new guide.

My father was thrilled. "My *amigos* call me Rafael!"

"And I am your *amigo*," Rafael agreed gamely, knowing that he had my father just where he wanted him.

Most people have built-in stranger danger radar. From a very young age, it's drilled into us that we shouldn't talk to them, eat their candy, or get in their beat-up van with the blacked-out windows. My father must have missed all those public service announcements because he seemed to be attracted to stranger danger. In fact, he thrived on it.

Deep-sea fishing in a flimsy canoe with a crazy German guy he had met just hours earlier? Did it. Whisking his family off to a remote island in a plane held together by duct tape to watch people throw themselves off a tower in the middle of the jungle? Yep, did that, too. Watch while a modern-day witch doctor packed his son full of narcotics in the South Pacific? Of course.

So, in a way, this turn of events was no surprise. That didn't stop my mother from trying to mitigate the potential damage. With a few years of Spanish lessons under her belt, my mother decided now would be a good time to put her language skills to use, perhaps hoping to convince Rafael that we were not ignorant American tourists who were easy marks for whatever scam he was cooking up.

"Hola, Rafael. Much gusto. Donde esta el hotel? Estamos muy cansados."

Rafael raised his left eyebrow in surprise, but that didn't stop him from pushing ahead with whatever racket he was running. "I'm sure you are tired, *mi amiga,*" he smiled. "Let me take your bags."

He trotted off with my mother's pink and black polka-dotted bag, leaving the rest of us to fend for ourselves. Soon enough we were zipping into town in Rafael's seen-better-decades Land Rover. The roughly paved streets of Puerto Ayacucho paired with the total lack of shocks or seatbelts in our transportation made us bounce up and down like a set of mismatched Whac-A-Moles. Between hitting our heads on the roof and slamming back down into our seats, it was hard to see where we were going.

Ralph and Rafael were deep in discussion in the front, but I couldn't hear a thing over the roar of the motor and the air rushing in the open windows. After a few minutes, the violent jouncing came to a sudden and unexpected halt, throwing us against the front seats.

"We're here," Rafael announced unnecessarily as he beamed back at us.

Disentangling ourselves from one another and grabbing our luggage, we turned to survey the besty that Puerto Ayacucho had to offer. Apparently "besty" meant something else in Spanish – maybe "crap palace" – because the Hotel Gran Amazonas was a decaying remnant of colonialist grandiosity that looked like a minor ground tremor or a good strong push would bring on its demise.

"You will like it very much," Rafael assured us all as we walked into the lobby. "There's a pool."

While my father checked us in, my mother, sister, and I went to check out the courtyard where the pool was located. Murky shamrock green with an unidentified fungi growing at its edges, it probably concealed a bevy of murdered tourists in its depths.

My mother cocked her head, clearly looking for a silver lining so she could put a positive spin on it. "It's quite...primitive," she finally ventured.

"I didn't want to go swimming anyway," I offered. I could tell my mother was trying to make the best of a bad situation. It wasn't her fault that we were here. Dad was the lone star of that blame game.

She brightened. "Maybe there will be other opportunities. Who knows what this trip has in store?"

We got an inkling of what might be in store when we rejoined the two Rafaels, who had retired to the hotel bar for a couple of cocktails. Rafael was in the midst of pitching my father on a scheme so ludicrous I knew instantaneously it would appeal to him.

"Mi amigo, I will take you up the Orinoco and the Rio Negro on a five-day expedition," Rafael explained as my father knocked back a scotch. "It is incredible!"

I knew nothing about the Orinoco other than what I had gleaned from the Enya song, which was that the river was calm and soothing, an experience akin to doing yoga in a candlelit studio or getting a massage by a blonde beauty with a cleavage-enhancing top. Something told me that Enya didn't have the full story though, especially when I considered its companion waterway.

Rio Negro means Black River, a phrase that did not inspire images of tranquility or sensuality. It sounded more like the setting for an Indiana Jones film or a place where a cult might commit group suicide. It's not a stretch of water that beckons you like a crystal-clear Caribbean cove; instead, it seemed to say, "Stay away. Very far away. Unless you have a death wish."

Oblivious of my inner monologue, Rafael continued his pitch to my father, having correctly guessed that Ralph was his easiest target and the keeper of the purse. The rest of us might as well have been invisible. I could tell my mother wanted to put an end to this line of thinking, but she was probably wondering how she would get Josephine and me home safely without my father's help. I wanted to tell her that we'd figure it out, just don't make us go on this damn fool's crusade.

175

Rafael didn't want to give the rest of us the time to rally our resources and put up a fight. "Do you like to fish?" he asked Dad. This guy was good. He clearly had Dad pegged.

"If I could spend every day fishing, I'd be happy," my Dad responded. "I'm missing some great ice fishing in upstate New York right now actually. Do you go ice fishing here?"

Rafael looked puzzled, "We have no ice, *señor.*" He chuckled. "We have something better though: piranhas!"

"Oooooh," my father exclaimed with an intrigued exhale as he hoisted his scotch to his lips. "I hear they make good eating."

"The very besty," Rafael assured him. "So you are in?"

"Absolutely!" my father agreed as he shook Rafael's hand exuberantly. Honestly, it was almost like the rest of his family weren't sitting next to him with "What the fuck are you doing?" looks on our faces. I would have bolted, but when you're in the middle of nowhere, the great irony is that there is nowhere to go.

My mother immediately saw the numerous pitfalls of such an ambitious plan, not the least of which was that it was literally misguided. She couldn't prevent that, but she could make sure we didn't starve. "We'll need to go food shopping tomorrow," she declared. "We're not going into the jungle without something to eat."

Dad seized on this idea. "We can spend the morning provisioning before we leave. I need to find a bottle of Glenlivet anyway."

This announcement implied my mother would be left to do all of the food shopping. I immediately began maneuvering for a way out of spending the morning perusing Venezuelan grocery stores with her. I trusted that she would do everything she could to ensure we survived this cockamamie scheme, but I didn't have much faith in either Rafael or Ralph doing the same.

Since we were sailing into the unknown, I figured it would fall on me to get something to save our asses when the going got tough.

176

Forgetting that blood made me queasy and hand-to-hand combat was not my forte, I latched onto the idea that some sort of locally made weaponry would be useful for fighting off bloodthirsty revolutionaries, bringing down capybaras or agoutis when our food supply ran out, and keeping Josephine in line.

"I'd love to go shopping with you, Dad," I volunteered. "Maybe we could look for some handicrafts to take home as souvenirs."

My father looked pleased that I wanted to come along, "Excellent. We'll make it a boys-only trip." Neither Jo nor my mother seemed disappointed at this turn of events, and so it was settled.

* * * * *

The following morning, the family divided along gender lines and embarked on our shopping expeditions. Rafael came with my father and me on our search for scotch and heavy-duty artillery, while my mother and sister paired up to tackle the massive grocery list we had written down on a combination of bar napkins and drink coasters.

Luckily, our triumvirate headed out on foot, so we were spared a brutal bouncing in Rafael's Land Rover. It was a beautiful day, and I could tell my father was exuberant. We were in an authentically remote location, there was a new adventure on deck, and he had a besty new friend to take him on a fishing expedition to a place that I was sure would be the ravenous maw of misfortune.

While the co-conspirators traded fishing stories, I took in Puerto Ayacucho. It could be the final stop in a lifelong journey of living beyond the edge.

From what I'd been able to glean from the few faded brochures scattered about the hotel lobby, Puerto Ayacucho was home to about 40,000 permanent residents. Several thousand native Indian commuters constantly flowed in from the surrounding rainforests, giving the small city the air of a 19th-century trading outpost.

Reinforcing this image were the numerous open-air markets we passed, which dazzled the senses with their riots of colors, sounds, and smells. They looked like the kind of places that Allan Quatermain did his shopping. Bizarre, spiny fruits were laid out on handwoven blankets, and old women with leathery, wrinkle-river faces hawked carved wooden statuettes from the recesses of narrow booths. Flashy green macaws fluttered spastically inside rusty cages, while mangy monkeys chained to vendors' tables screamed as we passed by and hungry dogs with bared teeth stalked every aisle.

At any store, stall, or blanket where they sold any type of foodstuff, my father would ask in broken Spanish for "Glenliveto." Then Rafael would smoothly ask using actual Spanish and the product's actual name. Neither tactic produced a bottle.

After the better part of three hours in search of the elusive Glenliveto – my father growing more frustrated and desperate at every new dead end – we finally found a dusty liquor store in the back corner of a market that stocked the prized liquor. There was only a single bottle left, half-hidden amidst a shelf full of rum. The proprietor, correctly surmising that the eager-eyed *tourista* before him would pay anything for the last scotch, used an exchange rate known only to highway robbers by immediately turning the faded price tag from Venezuelan *bolívares* into U.S. dollars.

My father didn't pause for a second. "Do you accept traveler's checks?"

"Yes, of course," replied the proprietor, the thought of the riches he was about to come into dancing before his eyes, "but there is a 20 percent convenience fee."

Out on the street a few minutes later, the bottle wrapped up in a brown paper bag, my father was on a high. "Now *this* is an adventure," he told me, clapping me on the back.

"So can we go looking for some souvenirs now?" I asked hopefully.

"Let's have a snack first," he replied as he all but skipped down the street, newly purchased bottle cradled lovingly in his arms.

178

He mimed shoveling food into his mouth. "Rafael, do you know a *buon ristorante* where we could eat?"

While Rafael spoke English well, he did not speak any Italian. That my father had just spoken Italian in a failed bid to try out his Spanish was not lost on either Rafael or me, though our guide was good-natured about it.

"*No problemo, Rafael Americano.*"

We ate in a little hole in the wall that was run by Rafael's brother or cousin or father-in-law; his explanation was lost in translation. Whoever he was, he and Rafael kept up a lively conversation in Spanish throughout the meal. My father pretended to understand what was going on by laughing loudly whenever one of them seemed to be delivering a punch line. This seemed to be most of the time judging by how much my father was chuckling.

We were set to rendezvous with my mother and Josephine early that afternoon, so my chance of acquiring protective weaponry was quickly slipping away. I didn't want to go into the jungle empty-handed. I was convinced that this military hardware was going to help me save my family from certain death and prove that beneath my pale, slightly pudgy exterior, I was a prince among warriors, a fighter so amazing that the local Ye'kuana Indians would adopt me as one of their own when they found me roaming the jungle. Once in the fold, I would be given a cool name like the Alabaster Prince of Death, and the tribal elders would sing of my awe-inducing deeds for millennia to come.

I knew my father wouldn't know the first thing about procuring royal armaments, so my only hope lay with Rafael. I had already determined that he was not the most dependable or trustworthy of souls, but sometimes you've just got to work with what you've got. When my father excused himself to go to the bathroom, I set my plan in motion.

"Rafael, you seem really well connected," I started. "I'm sure you know everyone around here."

"It's true. I know a lot of people," he said with the kind of braggadocio I was hoping for, "and a lot of people know Rafael."

The hook was in.

"Well, here's the thing. I want to bring home an authentic Ye'kuana bow-and-arrow set as a souvenir, but I don't think they sell them at the gift shop," I said. "If you can find my father a bottle of Glenliveto in this town, I know you can find anything."

Rafael pondered the compliment for a moment before smiling broadly. "I know somebody who might have one."

"Awesome!" I replied quickly as my father reappeared. "Hey, Dad, Rafael wants to take us over to his friend's house to show us some native arts made locally in the rainforest. Can we go before we have to meet up with Mom and Jo?"

He put down some bills to pay for the meal and picked up his bottle of precious scotch. "That sounds authentic. Why not?"

We ended up in the nondescript living room of a nondescript house on a nondescript side street. It didn't look promising at all. The house's owner, a middle-aged gringo wearing a faded guayabera shirt and a pair of khaki cargo shorts, was South America's answer to the Dude from *The Big Lebowski.* He greeted us enthusiastically with beery breath and slurred Spanish before scurrying off to the bowels of the house, where I could hear the strains of the Doors' "The End." It was definitely not as reassuring as an Enya song, not by a long shot.

When the amateur arms dealer returned, he was carrying a giant wooden bow and a quiver of arrows fletched with brightly colored feathers, probably poached from some endangered species.

"It isn't a toy," he warned me. "You can do some real damage with that thing."

I nodded as I turned the bow over in my hands. It was over three feet long, its bowstring so taut that I could barely pull it back an inch. The arrows could have easily taken down any threat short of a mastodon. According to the proprietor of this backwoods artillery depot, the Ye'kuana would sometimes dip the arrowheads into slow-acting poisons to ensure that their enemies died the most painful death possible.

"Don't worry. These aren't poisoned," he assured me.

This was definitely a step up from Gonzalo's gun in the Azores. I just hoped that if the occasion arose, I wouldn't freeze up again.

For some reason, my father wasn't concerned that I had just purchased a potentially lethal souvenir. Maybe he was already dreaming about fishing for piranha and enjoying a celebratory scotch. Whatever the case, I wasn't about to awaken his suspicions by revealing my true intent. All in all, things were looking pretty good. I was properly armed for the danger we were plunging into, and my chances of survival had just increased exponentially. The Alabaster Prince of Death was riding high.

My euphoria was short-lived. When we got back to the hotel, my mother and sister were already there waiting for us. Our luggage and bags of groceries littered the ground around them, sweat stains covered their clothing, and sunburns were starting to spread across their arms. In contrast, my Dad was carrying a lone bottle of scotch and I was wielding a lethal weapon. Neither of us had even begun to perspire.

"What the hell is that?" my mother asked, circling me in the same way a lion loops around its prey before ripping it to bloody bits.

"These arrows aren't the poisoned kind," I attempted to reassure her.

Clearly, it was the wrong thing to say.

She turned to confront my father, pinning him with her gimlet stare. "Ralph, what were you thinking?"

My father shrugged, giving our guide a pat on the back. "Don't worry, Alison. A friend of Rafael's got them for us. They're perfectly safe."

181

Rafael suddenly recalled that he had something to do out at the car and beat a hasty retreat. My father rather heroically stood his ground by pretending to ignore the poisoned arrows my mother's eyes were shooting at him.

"Give those to me," my mother ordered in a thunderous voice that assured me that the consequences of my failing to do what she had asked would be more dire than taking a poisoned quill to the chest. And so, the Alabaster Prince of Death meekly handed over his bow and arrows to the Supreme Goddess of You'll Do What I Tell You Right Now.

Didn't she know she had just sealed our fate? We might as well ask Rafael for four coffins right now because I saw this trip ending with a group funeral.

"Now that that is taken care of," my mother said in a voice that brooked no argument, "let's get going."

After loading our supplies into Rafael's Land Rover and my bow and arrows in the dumpster behind the hotel, we headed off down a muddy road that cut through the countryside. We were to board our boat at the end of the rapids that divided the Orinoco outside Puerto Ayacucho, presumably to avoid these more dangerous waters.

As we drove along, Rafael kept hyping our trip. "You will never forget it. I can promise you that!"

My mother sighed. "Yes, Rafael. If it's anything like our trip to Los Roques, I'm sure we won't."

I knew with the utmost certainty that Rafael and my mother were right when we got down to the dock and beheld the boat we'd be taking. It wasn't a ferry, a yacht, or even a raft befitting Huck Finn. Instead, our transportation was a skinny wooden boat about 18 feet long, not even as wide as a compact car. A rusty corrugated tin roof had been slapped on top to provide a modicum of cover from whatever the Amazon threw at us. I doubted it would shield us from even the mildest of thunderstorms or stave off the swarms of vampire bats I imagined roamed freely in the heart of darkness where we were headed.

Venezuelans generously refer to these scrappy vessels as *casa flotantes*, which translates literally to "house boats," though I believe the alternate translation is "Where am I going and why am I in this handbasket?"

My mother didn't say anything as her eyes took in our transportation, but her shoulders slumped resignedly.

Rafael introduced us to our boatman, a swarthy, dark-eyed native who spoke no English except "I José. Like José Canseco."

He seemed nice enough, and he helped us load our luggage and supplies on board before heading to the back of the boat to putter with the motor.

"He's getting it in the besty shape possible," Rafael reassured us when we looked back at Like José Canseco feverishly fiddling with an oily gasket on the outboard motor at the back.

However, it didn't sound like it was in the besty shape when we pulled away from the dock 15 minutes later. The motor immediately begin to cough and sputter like someone choking on a chicken bone while having a heart attack. It was hard to concentrate on the lush landscape gliding by us as the little Yamaha kept belching up black smoke and diesel. To further distract us, Like José Canseco started swearing as if he were Like Scarface.

"*Puta! Merde! Coño!*" he bellowed.

Josephine and I quickly mimicked him. "*Puta! Merde! Coño!*" we gleefully chanted, ignorant of what we were saying but relishing the power the words seemed to have.

We were enjoying it too much because my mother, who spoke excellent Spanish, could hear us over the constant backfires from the failing motor. "Stop that right now," she reprimanded with a sharp shake of her head and finger. "Or else I'm going to ask Rafael to leave you over there on the shore."

That threat kept us quiet until the bugs started biting a little while later. I'm not talking about an occasional nibble; it was if our boat were being dive bombed by every mosquito in the Amazon Basin.

My father was the first to let another obscenity slip out. "Jesus fucking Christ," he exclaimed, slapping his bare neck and arms where they were being attacked by kamikaze mosquitoes.

"Ralph," my mother chastised him as she whacked her own pale arms. "Language."

"Little goddamn bastards," he continued before a sharp look from my mother reduced further profanities to incomprehensible muttering.

My sister and I would have echoed Dad if my mother hadn't been there, but we had to just grunt and bear it. We were outnumbered. A family of four pale-skinned Americanos against millions of mosquitoes was a losing proposition. Suddenly, I felt a great empathy for General Custer.

That, of course, is when the motor gave an ominous fart and went silent. We all paused from our swearing, swatting, and scratching to look back at the end of the boat where Rafael and the boatman were conferring.

"Don't worry," Rafael assured us with an ivory grin before completely not reassuring us. "Do you have a screwdriver by any chance, Señor Martell?"

Luckily, Dad carried a Leatherman wherever he went, but he was the only one who was ever allowed to use it. It was his baby. Many times I had asked to borrow it only to be denied because "you'll just chip the blade." But out here – miles from a hardware store and with no other option – the Leatherman was reluctantly handed over. The jerry rigging commenced anew as my father looked on anxiously and interjected at regular intervals, "Watch the blade! That's an expensive knife."

As Rafael and Like José Canseco jammed the Phillips-headed blade into the dark crannies of the engine, they exchanged short bursts of

Spanish. Rafael sounded both confused and angry while his boatman sounded resentful and annoyed. Meanwhile, the boat began to drift back the way we had come.

"This is the *problemo*," Rafael finally announced as a sheared pin was extracted from the dark depths of the outboard and held up triumphantly. Unsurprisingly enough, it turned out that this particular vessel didn't come with a spare-parts kit, so Rafael was forced to fashion a new pin out of a rusty nail he pried from the roof of the boat.

His MacGyver-esque endeavors were only partially successful: The motor returned to life but at one-tenth of its original power. Rafael assured us that we would be able to repair the boat at a Salesian mission that night. In keeping with the foreboding names the region was apparently known for, our destination was on Isla Raton – Island of the Rats.

Our blunted progress did have one upside: It allowed me to truly appreciate the strange alternate universe my father had crashed-landed us in. The river was an inky green, and the sunlight seemed to get swallowed up in it. The jungle came right up to the water's edge, a camouflage of greens, browns, and blacks. Years later, whenever I came across Werner Herzog's *Fitzcarraldo* on cable, I'd flinch as the camera panned across the dark jungle shores slipping past. In that grim vision, I saw what the jungle was capable of doing to men, what it had been capable of doing to my family.

Afternoon became evening as we inched along at a sluggard's pace. Whenever we would ask Rafael how close we were to the island, he'd answer "*una hora.*" By the fourth time we asked the question, we realized that "*una hora*" actually meant "we'll get there when we get there, so calm the fuck down."

Night fell and the moon rose, casting a ghostly glimmer on the water beside us. The boat cut a dark wound in the silvery surface and left fractured reflections in our pitiful wake, like we were slicing into the very essence of the river. On either side of us, the forest was an impenetrable wall. I stared at it intently, hoping to see what was hiding in its depths. It was fruitless; my eyes could only detect inky blackness.

There was an onslaught of strange sounds: querulous warbles, high-pitched shrieks, and deep-throated ribbits that rose and fell in a haunting, rhythmic pattern. It was so foreign; I had never heard anything quite like it. It was unsettling because I didn't know what made the sounds or how the creatures behind them might feel about our invasion of their homeland.

Jo and I both crouched down as low as we could in our seats, our primal instincts reminding us that the smaller a target is, the harder it is to hit. Mom and Dad sat silently near the front of the boat. Every time my father would try to speak, my mother would suddenly remember that she wanted to pull something out the depths of her bag, effectively shutting down the conversation.

A little after 10 o'clock, we finally pulled up to Isla Raton. There was no one around and a single dim light flickered near the end of the dock, so it almost didn't feel like we had reached civilization. That feeling didn't change when Rafael directed us down a short dirt path to the sloppily cleared dirt space that would serve as our campground. He helped us sling up our hammocks with mosquito-netting enclosures then disappeared. I felt like I was being left as an offering on the altar of some strange god.

Everyone else zonked out almost instantly. I nodded off quickly, but I jolted awake just a few minutes later.

What was that? There was a weird sound. Shit, there was nothing but weird sounds. What could it be? The rats? God, I hated rats.

I lay there suspended above the earth – the hammock slowly rocking from my fearful trembling – listening intently, but the only sound I could positively identify was my father's snores. Nothing happened, so I dozed off again. But every few minutes I would wake up, convinced I heard something scratching and snuffling in the darkness near me.

The rats were everywhere; I could sense them. I kept peering into the void, looking for their gleaming eyes or the flash of teeth. I envisioned them as more vicious versions of the gruesome beasts I was convinced lived in my closet when I was two. Here I was 15 years later still afraid of monsters in the dark.

At least they can't get up to me in the hammock. Unless…no, could it be possible? What if they somehow climbed down the rope from a tree, like a squirrel shimmying along a branch to score access to the bird feeder? That was not a comfortable thought to have in the middle of the Amazon at midnight.

The rest of the night was divided between thinking about how it would feel to be eaten alive by rats and dreaming about being eaten alive by rats.

I was surly and thoroughly disgruntled come morning. Rafael seemed to have had no problem sleeping through the impending rodent invasion. He was chipper and raring to go, while I could barely keep my eyes open. To say that I resented his *joie de vivre* would have been an understatement.

"We have a new engine," Rafael announced like Barnum presenting Houdini. "And you will fish today, *señor!*"

This perked my Dad up, but it didn't do much for me. I had no protection, and we were about to willfully interact with predatory fish that were genetically hardwired to kill.

Sounds like a fucking blast, Rafael!

We didn't linger on the island to seek out its namesakes; we just got into our cramped canoe of a boat and resumed our journey. An hour later, my father and Rafael joined me in the prow of our slender craft while my mother and sister huddled to read in the meager shade of the roof.

"This is the besty place for the piranha," Rafael announced, looking just as certain as when he had told us that the Gran Amazonas was the besty hotel ever. I was far from convinced and looking around dubiously for signs of the fanged fish, but the black waters seemed devoid of life.

"How do you know they're out there?" I asked. "It looks pretty quiet to me."

Rafael smiled in the smug way favored by villains contemplating the deaths of their archenemies. "Watch this."

He reached into a nearby ice chest and pulled out a pair of raw chicken breasts. Without any fanfare, he threw them off our starboard bow. It was like he had dropped depth charges.

Boom! Boom!

The water frothed up into a white maelstrom. I could see the occasional flash of a fish, but it was over so quickly that it was hard to tell what I was looking at. The one thing that did register were the sets of small, sharp teeth tearing apart the chicken breasts in a carnivorous frenzy. This may look cool when you're watching it on Animal Planet from the comfort of your couch, but it's not so cool when you could fall into it.

My father loved it. "I bet a lot of guys don't go fishing naked for those suckers!"

Rafael didn't bother to laugh at my father's half-witticism. Instead, he handed us both fishing poles baited with chunks of chicken. "Good luck, *mis amigos.*"

I'm certain my father and I interpreted this differently.

We took up positions on either side of the boat and began casting. Since I had seen what those teeth could do to a chicken breast, I didn't want one of those little bastards to think that my thumb was a drumstick. Because my father would not interrupt his own fishing to help untangle my lines, I thought it best to keep fouling my reel. This effectively sidelined me from the blood sport and kept me in a piranha-free zone.

Every once in a while, I would shout over an encouraging word to my father, as much to distract him from my own lack of progress as to keep his spirits up. "Way to go, Dad!" I yelled as I pretended to cast my line. "You're on fire."

On the other side of our barely seaworthy *casa flotante*, my father was having the time of his life. He probably wasn't even aware that his family was with him because he was pulling in piranhas at a feverish pace. Hauling the writhing and enraged fish on board, he'd throw them on the deck and quickly kill them with a sharp blow or two from a gore-covered hammer that Rafael had left out for this very purpose. Once their brains were splattered mulch, he'd safely get the hook out of their mouths and throw the fish into the cooler.

My father was a striking figure that day. From the single-minded focus with which he caught and cudgeled the piranha to his ridiculous get-up, he drew your eye. For this leg of the journey, he had embraced the horrors of Tarponwear sporting gear with a zeal that doubtless had the product team in Jackson Hole, Wyoming, rubbing their hands in avaricious glee as they looked at their profit statement.

In those days, Tarponwear was touted with a lot of ®s and ™s in the description. Its creators promised that it was a technologically advanced fabric that would revolutionize the fishing experience for true enthusiasts. Unfortunately for my father, Tarponwear only seemed to come in unfathomably repugnant colors – dead salmon, limpid blue, anemic taupe. Draped in these heinous shades, he stood out against the backdrop of the black river and the rich green jungle.

My father neither noticed nor cared about his lack of fashion sense. After a couple of hours, he had amassed a trove of piranhas that would have fed an entire tribe of Ye'kuana, while I had yet to land a single one. It wasn't until he took a break to crack open a beer that he finally realized I had not contributed to our dinner plans. He seemed surprised.

"All you have to do is throw your line out and Mother Nature does the rest," he told me as he took my pole from me and started to untangle the line. "I almost feel guilty about how easy it is."

With a few deft movements, he undid my hours of piranha avoidance. "Here you go. Give it a try now."

"Gee, thanks, Dad," I said as I reluctantly took back the pole. "You're a real savior. I don't know what went wrong."

He gave me a jarring clap on the back. "Good luck!"

I made a move as if to cast again, but thanks to a bit of *deus ex machina*, my mother interrupted us with the news that it was lunchtime. I took this legitimate excuse to drop my pole and zip to the back of the boat as quickly as possible.

Underneath the meager overhang, she had spread out a simple lunch of ham and cheese sandwiches, crispy homemade plantain chips from the market, and freshly cut mango slices. There were cold Cerveza Polar beers for my father and nonalcoholic, root beer-ish Maltín Polar for the rest of us. I quickly made up a plate and dove right in.

My mother desperately wanted to bring some normalcy to this clearly unorthodox experience, so she tried to kick-start a casual lunchtime conversation.

"Did you catch anything, Nevin?"

I didn't have a chance to answer before my father piped up.

"No, he didn't. I caught several dozen though."

"My line kept getting tangled," I protested.

"Well, then you should have untangled it." He took a long sip of beer. "Don't you ever pay attention when I'm teaching you how to properly use a rod?"

"Of course, Dad," I said, wishing I was screaming, "Did you see what those little bastards did to the chicken breasts?!!?"

"It's not that difficult. You just need to use your head." He helpfully pointed at his own as if I might be so slow that I wouldn't have caught his drift otherwise.

"Maybe next time," my mother chirped in an effort to save our lunch.

"Right," said Dad with the kind of tone that said he didn't believe I'd ever possess the wits required to be anything more than ballast in this *casa flotante*. "Well, I hope you don't spend your whole life wishing you had seized this moment."

With that final pronouncement-turned-jab, he took his plate and headed to the far back where Rafael and Like José Canseco were enjoying a liquid lunch. I was off the hook and my extremities were safe, so I took myself to a shaded corner at the fore of the boat and happily buried myself in *The Return of the King*.

For a few hours, I was able to ignore everything around me and didn't surface from J. R. R. Tolkien's ring-obsessed alternate universe until we'd stopped to make camp for the night. My father interrupted my preferable-to-reality reading session with a bark. "Give us a hand unloading."

Putting the book down on the deck with a grumpy slap, I clambered to my feet. "Sure, Ralph."

After ordering me to do his bidding, my father immediately disembarked and pretended to be so deeply involved in a personal survey of the local flora that he couldn't help with the unpacking himself. Since my mother and sister had scampered off into the jungle for an untimely bathroom break, it fell on me to do all the work.

There was a huge problem with the whole situation: There was no dock. Apparently, the locals don't go up and down the rarely traveled portions of the Orinoco to install piers where weary travelers could tie up.

This meant I had to jump from the prow of our shaky *casa flotante* to the land, which was a tricky proposition. There were approximately three to six feet between the launching pad and terra firma, depending on where the river's current dragged the boat on its mooring line, so I had to carefully gauge each leap.

I knew there was a school of piranhas just beneath us waiting to strip the pale flesh from my bones to avenge their brethren who'd fallen to my father's hook. I had to be very careful. The possibility that I might look like the bleached skeleton that hung in a biology classroom wasn't an exciting proposition.

Damn Jo and her elfin bladder. She was dexterous and coordinated, whereas I had earned the tongue-in-check nickname Poetry in Motion from a track and field coach because my running style resembled a blind antelope with broken legs trying to scramble out of a tar pit.

Though the stakes were high, my process for avoiding death by carnivorous fish was ridiculously straightforward. I'd bring whatever I was carrying to the front of the boat, wait a moment to gauge if it was going to move farther or closer to the shore, then step back, sprint forward, and jump with my fingers mentally crossed.

Every time I made it to the other side of this watery Death Valley, I dreamed up a new way I would someday make Dad pay for this. I would shut him in a drawer full of ravenous gerbils. Or maybe douse him head to toe in pollen then break a beehive over his head. Or maybe I would slip a few dozen scorpions into his sleeping bag the next time we went camping. If there was a next time, I reminded myself. We had to make it out of the Amazon alive first.

Hoping Jo would show up and take over the unloading process, I made sure to take my time. Each trip to the shore only included a couple of items – maybe a small bag of rice and a stick of butter for Rafael, who was busy filleting and seasoning the piranhas my father had caught.

The unpacking moved as quickly as molasses in wintertime, but despite my worst intentions, I was finally left with nothing but the bottle of Glenlivet my father desired above all else. I picked it up and made my way to the prow. Looking down, I thought I could see the flash of incisors in the murky green of the water.

Fuck it. Hopefully, I'll look back at this and laugh. I took a deep breath, got a running start, and leapt into the chasm.

As soon as I jumped, I knew something was going wrong. I was sailing toward the shore, but my precious passenger was bailing out. My fingers grasped uselessly for the bottle, but there was nothing there but air. In the space between the prow and the riverbank, time stopped. I looked down and saw the bottle of Glenlivet tumbling down toward the water, end over end in super slow motion.

"Noooooo," I heard myself say, the word so stretched out that it sounded more like a moan.

I saw my whole life flash before my eyes – a fast-forwarded parade of unfashionable outfits, strange explorations, and weird encounters, but no girlfriends. For all that I'd done and all the places I'd been, this high-speed miniature movie was depressingly short. It felt unfinished, and I didn't want it to end there and then. Where was the heartwarming scene with the big swelling musical number as I ride off into the sunset with my beautiful damsel in search of further adventures?

My dreams of a Hollywood ending were abruptly cut short when the bottle hit the water, I tumbled onto the shore in a scotch-less heap, and I heard my father roar all in the same moment. For a second, I was tempted to dive into the river as much to retrieve the Glenlivet as to get away from my father. But then I remembered the piranhas.

I scrambled up into an awkward crouch and swiveled toward my father, who was standing over me in a bloodthirsty rage.

"What. The. Fuck. Was. That?" he spat out.

His face was flushed, and his eyes were bulging. I hadn't seen him this angry since I'd thrown rocks through the walls of our glass greenhouse when I was four.

"Uhhh, ummm." I looked toward the heavens for help, but God must have been on a bathroom break with my mother and sister because no one answered my desperate prayers.

As I babbled nonsense, questions flashed through my mind. Did they have 911 in the Amazon? What would my classmates say in their eulogies? Would my parents bury or cremate me?

Dad had no time for such sputtering inaction. "Get it out. Now!" He pointed toward the river's depths, his arm shaking with anger. Jesus, he was serious. This was bad.

I had one small question. It was a minor point really, but there were major consequences for me. Perhaps he was simply overlooking it in his desire to have a glass of scotch. "But what about the piranhas?"

He snorted. "Piranhas don't drink scotch. I do."

Looking around at the piles of luggage I had just unloaded, he started opening bags and throwing out pieces of clothing. "Where's your snorkeling gear? Put it on and get in there."

I gulped and stared. Even though the water was only five or six feet deep where the Glenlivet had fallen, it seemed like I was staring into the deepest abyss in the world. I had read enough Jules Verne books and *Amazing Adventures* comics to know that if I dove in, I'd never surface again.

Remember the chicken breasts.

I didn't know what to do. My father looked ready to kill me if I stayed on shore, and the piranhas would surely kill me if I went in the water. I eyed the jungle, only 20 feet away.

I could make a break for it and survive in the wilds of the Amazon. I would live off the land, befriend the Ye'kuana, and train a hawk to help me hunt like I was living out *My Side of the Mountain*. There was still a chance for me to become the Alabaster Prince of Death.

Thankfully, that fate was averted. Having heard my father's shouts, my mother raced over. Praise God!

"What is going on here? Is everything okay?" She looked me up and down to see if there were broken bones sticking through the skin or blood gushing from an open wound.

"He's fine, but my Glenlivet isn't," Dad huffed. "It's on the bottom of the goddamn river. He's going in after it."

Mom stepped between us. "With the piranhas?"

My point exactly!

That didn't give my father pause. "It's safe enough."

My mother's voice took on a low, steely tone, and her hands went up, part scolding him, part blocking him. "He's not going in that river, Ralph."

"Goddamn it, Alison…." he trailed off, as if not sure how to follow it up. Then he turned back to me. "You're not a little kid anymore. It's time to grow up and act like a man."

Turning on his heel, he stalked off toward the fire where Rafael and Like José Canseco were pretending they weren't listening.

"Whatever," I muttered quietly enough so he couldn't hear me. I didn't care what he said because I was alive.

My mother put a hand on my shoulder. "Are you all right?"

I shook her off as I stood up. "Yeah, I'm just fucking peachy."

"Don't talk like that to me."

She looked so hurt I immediately regretted I had turned my anger on my savior. "Sorry, Mom."

"It's okay." She tried to give me a hug, but I wasn't interested in going that far. I squirmed away and stalked off to the edge of the campsite. Jo was already sitting there.

"You're not going swimming?" she tried joking.

"He can kiss my ass," I muttered as I squatted on the ground next to her. "Is he crazy?"

She shrugged. "Classic Dad. Remember that time he chased you down the street with the rake last fall because you wouldn't help clean up the lawn?"

"Like I could forget it. He wasn't too happy with you either because you were talking back to him."

"Oh yeah. I thought he was going to totally rip my head off."

"Well, we survived," I said with a humorless laugh.

She nodded. "Just so we end up in the middle of the Amazon with a bunch of maniacs and killer fish."

"Yeah, it's fucking insanity."

We lapsed into silence, and I began imagining how this trip might end. I was caught between two nightmarish scenarios: fish eating me alive and my father flaying me alive.

When my mother called us all for dinner at the campfire, Dad didn't say a word to me. Instead, he chose to sullenly stare into the flickering flames, as if his longing would conjure his precious bottle from the depths of the Orinoco. I kept the fire between us in case he felt the need to throttle me as a way of working through his loss. Even Rafael serving the piranha didn't buoy his spirits.

"They're boney" was all Dad said as he sucked the flakey white flesh off the carcass. They tasted like salvation to me, but I kept my mouth shut.

* * * * *

The next day, I continued to stay as far away from my father as our little boat would allow. I crouched in the prow while Dad told Rafael about his last trip to South America before he had a family, which he kept saying "went so much smoother than this one." Sensing my father's dissatisfaction, Rafael tried to placate him with the promise of warm beds, hot food, and ice-cold drinks – "maybe even Glenlivet" – in Colombia that evening.

A few *una horas* later, we pulled up to our destination. At least there was a dock at this stop, but it was the most uninviting anchorage in the world. A soldier in dusty olive fatigues stood at the end of it, smoking a cigarette while his machine gun hung by his side. He gave us a half-interested look that was somewhere between "I am looking forward to defiling your women" and "Do I need a reason to kill you?" that my father either missed or chose to ignore.

"*Hola, señor,*" Dad greeted him with a hearty wave.

The guard nodded back. "*Hola.*"

He took a final drag on his cigarette, dropped it to the dock, and ground it out with his black military boots that had probably been polished by the little fingers of local children before he shot them all to death. Without another word, he turned around and ambled back toward the unappealing town behind him, which might as well have had a giant neon sign over it flashing "You will die here."

Rafael seemed to think that all was as it should be and cheerily started lifting our bags from the boat as he talked up the "most besty accommodations" that awaited us in what I was beginning to think could be my final resting place.

"This is the worsty place ever," I whispered to my sister, who sniggered loudly.

Though we had been to the bottom of some hellholes before, this marked a new low. Even Los Roques would have been preferable. Here the streets were unevenly paved with well-worn cobblestones smeared with dirt, oil, and what looked like blood. Trash was strewn everywhere like it was an aesthetic choice. Buildings ran together so I felt like I was walled in on either side. There weren't a lot of people around, but those who did pass by or peer out from windows gave us looks of curiosity or disdain, as if we were unwelcome trespassers.

No one spoke as we wove our way through the village. I wasn't sure if it was because we were all shell-shocked by this new environment or because we were afraid of upsetting the locals by saying something unintentionally offensive, which would, of course, result in us being lined up against a wall and summarily executed.

My low opinion of our latest pit stop didn't change when we got to the barn-turned-derelict-guesthouse that Rafael had been heavily promoting. What little paint remained was peeling off the weatherworn siding, the front door hung lopsided in the frame, and the yard was filled with gutted car frames that looked like they had been repeatedly firebombed. I didn't mean to sound ungrateful after the mosquitoes, rats, and piranhas, but it was a hellhole of epic proportions.

"Puta! Merde! Coño!" Jo muttered, and for once, my mother didn't silence or correct her.

Dad just stared at it balefully, as if he couldn't imagine why Lady Luck had dealt him such an abominable hand.

"Come in, come in," Rafael urged since we all seemed to be holding back.

We reluctantly followed him, delicately sidestepping the car carcasses, which I peered into to see if there were any human bodies inside. They were filled mostly with ochre rust-covered parts. The bodies are probably in the trunk; that's where gangsters always put the dead guys. Actually, I was pretty sure that's where Dad would stuff me if he had the chance.

The inside of the house wasn't much of an improvement. The small, windowless room where I would be spending the night seemed to have a thin layer of dust on every surface, though I didn't see any rat holes in the wainscoting. At least the lack of windows meant that the soldier from the dock couldn't crawl in under the cover of darkness and slit my throat. He'd have to come through the door, which I already planned on barricading with the bed and the wobbly dresser in the corner. If only I had my bow and arrows.

Jo joined me a moment later. "This place freaks me out."

"Tell me about it. Will you give me a hand with this dresser? I'm going to block the door with it later."

"Good idea," said Jo as she picked up the other end and we shuffled over toward the doorway. "I can't wait to leave."

"Me either. This is definitely one for the record book where they keep track of all the crappy records that people don't want to break."

Jo smiled. "Worst Vacation Ever!"

"Most Deadly Swimming Spot," I added.

"Tour Guide of the Year," she quipped. "Not."

"Top Destination for Rat Lovers!"

We pushed the dresser against the wall by the doorway and paused. Once again, here we were at the end of the world. I felt a huge rush of gratitude that Jo was there, and let her know this in the only way my teenage bravado would allow.

"You can read my *Rolling Stone* if you want. I'm done with it anyway."

She looked surprised, but she took it. "Thanks. Do you want to read my *Seventeen?*"

"Nah, I'm still only halfway through *The Return of the King*. It's kinda boring though. A lot of walking."

"Whatever. That's what you get for reading a book about midgets with hairy feet."

I tried not to sound too offended. "They're hobbits."

"Yeah, whatever. Anyway, thanks for the magazine."

She disappeared out the door, and I flopped down on the bed to get back to Frodo and Sam's endless jaunt across Mordor. The unforgiving wastelands, coupled with the constant fear of countless enemies and the danger of an untimely death at every turn, was a truly unenviable situation for the two hobbits. At least they had each other.

I made it through a couple more chapters before my mother popped her head around the door. "Dinner time."

"Please tell me we're not eating piranha again." I put down my book.

That earned a smile. "No, there's actually a restaurant in town."

"A Michelin three-star, I'm sure."

"Stop it," but I could tell she was amused. "You're on very thin ice with your father right now."

"Whatever. He is being ridiculous. Did he really think I was going to swim with a bunch of piranhas just so he could have a cocktail?"

She sat down on the bed next to me. "Don't think for an instant that this is my ideal vacation. You know I'd be very happy reading a book on a quiet little beach."

"So why are we in the middle of the Amazon with a couple of guys who will probably get us killed?"

There was a pause. When she spoke, she talked slowly, as if to ensure that every word was the right one. "Sometimes in a marriage you have to go along with what your spouse wants or give them something you don't want to surrender, even if it's not what you would choose to do if you were on your own. Someday when you have a family, you'll know what I mean."

I had seen my father give my mother plenty of generous gifts, but it sounded like something intangible was missing from those exchanges. She took a deep breath and patted me on the knee. "I'll see you outside in 15 minutes."

When we gathered in front of the Shitz-Carlton – or maybe it was the Discomfort Inn – my father looked defeated and dejected. It was like a giant hand had punched him in the stomach, expelling every last ounce of adventurousness in one whoosh. For once, he didn't say a word as we walked through town.

When we arrived at the rundown café where we would be dining, I felt almost equally overcome. Not even a generous guidebook writer would have been able to summon a "quaint" or a "rustic" to describe this dingy dive. The tables were covered with well-worn sheets of yellowing plastic that sported endless stains, still-fresh puddles of dark sauces, and dried clumps of rice, which looked like dead maggots. A half-lit Budweiser sign flickered over the bar, where an aging Colombian with slicked-back graying hair and a damp rag slung over his left shoulder stood with his arms crossed like a surly bouncer.

Two soldiers in crusty fatigues sat sipping beers while they watched a Latin American game show zigzagged with bad-reception static. They paused for a minute to measure us up before returning their attention to the cleavage-heavy hostess on television.

A worse-for-the-wear waitress waddled out of the kitchen reeking of a bracingly floral perfume. She turned to my father as if he was the only one present.

"*Hola. Cerveza?*"

"Scotch?" he asked hopefully.

"*No, señor. Cerveza?*" She handed him a menu, which looked like it was covered in the same saffron-shaded plastic as the table.

"Okay," my father agreed, unsurprised by the lack of fine spirits but still thoroughly disappointed.

The waitress was about to walk away when my mother interjected. "*Tres bottelas de agua, por favor.*"

The waitress gave her a curt nod and moved away toward the bar.

"Ralph, do you want to tell them or should I?"

He looked up gloomily. "You do it."

Mom swiveled so she was facing Jo and me. "Your father and I have decided that we're going home tomorrow. Isn't that right, Ralph?"

She shot him a look, and he nodded curtly. Clearly, I was not the only one she had talked to back at the guesthouse.

"According to Rafael, we might even be able to make the trip back to Puerto Ayacucho in a day because we're heading downstream," she continued. "We'll fly home on the first available flight."

We might be in Clinton in 36 hours? Halle-fucking-lujah! No more piranhas, no more *casa flotante*, no more Rafael, and no constant threats of unusual death. Thank you, Mom!

I had to wonder though: How had it come to this? When I was younger, our vacations were far-out and far off the beaten path but fun. Though we sometimes found ourselves in perilous situations, it was because of outside forces – a depressurized plane or one held together with duct tape – not because of internal strife.

Maybe we had stretched our limits beyond the breaking point. We had unknowingly crossed that invisible line that divides safety and sanity from mayhem and madness.

Or maybe our family's current dysfunction was caused by the marital discord that had been slowly building between my parents. Her yin and his yang were clearly out of alignment, a slow decay that was suddenly only visible in hindsight. They had always found a way forward together before, but this time I wasn't so sure.

This trip had somehow irrevocably changed a crucial part of our family dynamic for all of us. The four of us didn't want to spend time together, even if we had been in paradise. It looked as if our adventures together had concluded. Unlike the Swiss family Robinson though, we weren't rescued at the end – we needed saving.

It Wasn't Like This the Last Time

[Costa Rica 2012, Age 38]

That trip to Venezuela and Colombia was one of our last together as a family. A little over a year after our surprisingly safe return, my parents announced that they were separating. They finalized their divorce several years later. Ultimately, they couldn't sustain the constant energy and emotion needed to keep our lovable freak show together. Some marriages fall apart because there isn't enough adventure; this one crumbled because there was too much.

After the separation, Jo and I would occasionally travel with my mother or father. I took a trip to Puerto Vallarta, Mexico, with my mother, sister, and another mother-daughter pair. All of the women had recently gotten out of messy relationships or were in the midst of extricating themselves from one. As the only male, I took a lot of heat for every guy on the planet.

Several years after that debacle, my sister and I headed to Cuba with Dad. This ill-advised expedition turned out to be equally torturous. The days were divided into extended periods of stultifying boredom followed by rapidly achieved extreme drunkenness at night, which cycled through to stomach-churning, head-breaking hangovers the next morning. There were some highlights: an epic concert by Buena Vista Social Club's Omara Portuondo in the shadow of a decaying fort; daiquiris at Hemingway's old haunt, La Floridita; and shopping in the open-air markets for subversive street art. However, most of the pictures of the trip capture my sister and I with awkwardly ersatz smiles plastered on our faces.

As the four of us got older though, we worked hard to forge healthy bonds. This created a new symmetry between us, which gave me the confidence to try traveling with my parents again. My first experiment was a trip with my mother to Oaxaca, Mexico, in 2008 for *Dia de los Muertos*, which turned out to be an unforgettable riot of color, culture, and cuisine – not to mention a great time for everyone involved. My sister joined us with her young daughter,

Florence, while I travelled with my fiancée, Indira.

After that trip, Indira and I continued to globe-trot. We went to Anguilla and Saba in the Caribbean on our honeymoon and later visited Hawaii and San Miguel de Allende, Mexico. In the spring of 2012, we had to start rethinking our future travel plans when the white plastic stick came back with a positive sign one day. Indira was carrying our first child.

I knew that when the baby joined us our lives would be changed irrevocably. Our responsibilities and schedule would change, making long family trips to faraway locales or epic solo excursions nearly impossible for the foreseeable future. Every decision would have to be made by answering just one question: "Is this the best choice for our family?"

I yearned for a last hurrah, one final grand expedition, a trip I could tell our kid about when I was older. I was contemplating how I might accomplish this while I was talking to my father on the phone one evening. In between catching me up on the weather – "Not bad for this time of the year" – and the number of fish he'd caught on his latest expedition on the pond in front of his waterfront cabin – "One bass, decent sized. He'll be good eating." – he mentioned that he was thinking of moving from his home in upstate New York to Costa Rica, which he had visited after he and my mother divorced. Even though he was 85 years old, he was considering making this ambitious move on his own.

I had been to the Rich Coast myself a decade earlier to do some volunteer work and had fallen in love with the country. My three-week sojourn was divided between the small town of Monteverde in the cloud forest and the beautiful-sounding-until-you-know-what-it-means Islas Murcielagos (Bat Islands). There I watched as a nest of several hundred sea turtles broke free of their shells, and I snorkeled alongside a pod of playful dolphins and gigantic manta rays with wingspans twice my height.

Despite my deep appreciation for Costa Rica, the idea of my father moving there to while away his final days sounded like a madcap scheme. I imagined him being robbed by *banditos*, getting torn apart by wild jaguars, or simply expiring prematurely because he was nowhere near a hospital. However, I knew if I told him I thought that a new life in Costa Rica was a bad idea, it would simply reinforce his resolve to do it. I'm sure he'd rib me. "Where's your sense of adventure, Nevin?"

That's when I had an epiphany.

"What if you and I went down to Costa Rica together?" I offered. "We could check out where you might live and get the lay of the land."

Then I channeled Rafael and set my hook. "We could even go fishing on Lake Arenal."

Dad's fond memories of bringing up more than his fair share of *guapote*, a cichlid fish with hypnotic spotting, and razor-toothed *machaca* had become one of his favorite tales to tell at family get-togethers, cocktail parties, and anywhere else he could find an audience.

"You're always telling me how many fish you caught there," I continued. "Unless, of course, you were exaggerating."

"Never let the truth get in the way of a good story," he half-joked. "Actually, that sounds like a great idea. Set it up."

This was a first. My father had never relinquished control of the vacation planning. Finally, I would be in charge of playing the cruise director. The captain's hat was being passed.

I set about making the necessary arrangements. I wanted my trip with my father to match the epic scope of both our memories of Costa Rica, so I started researching housing options, flights, ground transportation, and local attractions.

I dutifully bought a guidebook, read it from cover to cover, and tabbed down the items of interest. Numerous calls and emails were exchanged with landlords, rental car agencies, and fishing outfits. Specialty rainwear appropriate for a trip to the cloud forest was purchased. The GPS was loaded with up-to-date maps of Central America. I double-checked the particulars of my life insurance policy. A supply of Lärabars was stowed away in my backpack in case we found ourselves stranded in the middle of nowhere. I even lit a few Guadeloupe candles from the Spanish aisle of the grocery store, hoping to bring good luck to our trip.

After I had all the particulars lined up, I plotted out a detailed itinerary, which turned out to be for my peace of mind alone. I'm pretty sure the only part of it my father looked at was the departure information so he wouldn't miss his flight.

As our day of departure grew near, I found myself getting nervous. Would we drive each other crazy? How would the trip measure up against all our other crazy adventures? Would we catch any fish?

* * * * *

"It wasn't like this the last time I was here," my father harrumphed as we cast our lines toward the shallows of Lake Arenal.

It was easy to believe him. We'd been fishing for more than two hours, and there'd been nary a nibble. I didn't mind that we hadn't caught dinner yet. It was a sunny morning in early November. A few wispy clouds punctuated the blue sky, and a slight breeze ruffled the lake, keeping us cool. At the far southeastern end, a wall of mist obscured Arenal Volcano, an active peak that had had its last major eruption in 1998.

I wasn't sure that my father and I would ever have another day quite like this one. Although he was the most active and adventurous 85-year-old I knew, his hearing and eyesight had been slowly deteriorating in recent years, and he often got dizzy spells — aftershocks from a stroke a decade before.

"Let's try trolling," our guide, Sancho, suggested as he fired up the outboard motor at the end of his flat-bottomed johnboat.

He guided us away from the water's edge until we were 100 yards out, then angled us parallel to the jungle-covered shoreline. As we cast our lines on opposite sides, I mentally crossed my fingers in the hope that we would catch something. I didn't want this adventure to end in disappointment for my father, who clearly wanted to add some new myths to his storytelling arsenal.

"I've got something!" I heard him exclaim behind me. Unfortunately, when he pulled in his line, he found an immature, six-inch *machaca* wriggling at the end of it.

Thankfully, his next strikes yielded a pair of two-pound fish that were tossed into an ice chest after a few quick smacks to the head. After another hour, I managed to add another to our haul. It wasn't enough to brag about, but it was enough for dinner.

We arranged for the fish to be prepared at *El Establo* (The Stable), a rustic roadside restaurant and horse-rental operation that was a 10-minute drive from the villa we were renting. We were the only diners that evening, so we took over a long table near the open kitchen. The fish were washed, battered, and fried whole. They arrived on a plastic platter with a simple salad of lettuce leaves, tomato rounds, and cucumbers. The crisp salted skin paired well with the mild sweet meat, all washed down with rum and Cokes. It was a great meal, but it clearly didn't measure up to my father's expectations.

The next morning, his disillusionment was evident during breakfast at Tom's Pan German Bakery, a touristy but tasty outpost on the eastern edge of Nuevo Arenal, a tiny frontier-style town of just a little more than 2,000 residents. As we tucked into platters of fresh fruit and a basket of still-warm whole-wheat bread studded with seeds and grains, he griped through reminiscence.

"Twenty years ago, we were pulling fish out of the lake that were this big," he said, putting down his latte and holding his hands two feet apart. "We were throwing them back by the end of the day."

I nodded gamely, trying not to become frustrated with his comparison to a seemingly impossible-to-top experience. I realized in that moment that I, too, wanted to be able to talk about this trip in such legendary terms.

When I was young, I operated, like many children, under the wonderfully naive assumption that everything and everyone I knew would always be a part of my life. There would always be another trip to take with them, another adventure to be had. Growing older, watching family and friends slip off into the ether, has taught me otherwise.

As time with my father inexorably shrank, I found myself clinging ever more fiercely to the moments that we had together. The child in me believed that if I held on hard enough, maybe nothing would ever change. Listening to him live in the past made me feel as if he was ignoring the present. How could we have a new adventure together if he kept reliving the old ones?

After breakfast, he mentioned his dissatisfaction to our landlord, Glenn McBride, who had arranged our fishing expedition.

"You could always try Lago de Cote," Glenn mused. "But only locals go there."

That was all my father needed to hear. If there was one thing he would never stop craving on vacations, it was an authentic experience.

After Dad automatically agreed to the idea, I asked Glenn to give us a little more background. Just to the northwest of Nuevo Arenal, a heart-shaped lake is sunk into the center of an extinct volcano. The *guapote* and *machaca* are plentiful, and Glenn knew just the guide to take us — Jim Harvey.

Unfortunately, Jim could only take us on Friday – the day before we were due to leave. If we didn't catch anything then, I knew that I was going to hear about it on the plane ride home (and every time our trip came up in conversation). Worse still, we weren't going to have the adventure we were both seeking. This new turn of events left a couple of days open in my meticulously crafted itinerary, which I had assumed would be spent pulling dinners out of Lake Arenal.

We could drive up to Monteverde in the cloud forest," I suggested after Glenn had left. "It's a national park, so maybe we could go on a hike. I saw a toucan and rainbow-colored parrots the last time I was up there."

I could tell that this ornithological scenario wasn't enough of a draw for my father, who sipped his cup of morning joe instead of jumping at the opportunity. Once again, I conjured Rafael's huckster spirit.

"There's actually an amazing coffee roaster in Monteverde," I told him. "It has a little café attached to it where they make an incredible espresso."

Sure enough, that piqued his interest.

"That could be fun," he allowed. It might not be a fishing expedition, but it would do in a pinch.

* * * * *

Early the next morning, we fueled up our Toyota Land Cruiser Prado and began the four-hour journey. On our way out of town, we passed a wrecking ball-sized boulder on the side of the road. It had been crudely carved into a strange skull that looked like a simian crossed with an alien. It wasn't the most reassuring of omens.

Our trip took us eastward, along the northern shore of Lake Arenal. At the end, we followed the curve of the shore southward past the dormant volcano. Unable to resist the temptation to be tourists for a moment, we pulled over on a straightaway, where there was a stunning view of the fog-wreathed peak, to take a few photos. For the first time on a trip, I took more than my father in a single session. If my sister had been there, I'm sure I wouldn't have heard the end of it.

An hour or so later, the elevation began to grow steeper as we wended our way up the poorly maintained dirt roads into the national park surrounding the cloud forest. Fields and pastures gave way to heavily wooded stretches punctuated occasionally by a small village or a homestead.

"What's that?" my father asked as we approached a ramshackle barn-like structure on our right side with a primitive sign out front advertising fresh sugar cane juice.

I didn't come to Costa Rica armed with any assignments, but as a freelance writer passionate about food and travel, I was always looking for stories. This rustic roadside juice bar could be such an opportunity.

"I'm not entirely sure," I said as I pulled into the gravel driveway to park. "Let's check it out."

A man dressed in well-worn jeans and only a thin white T-shirt despite the damp chill in the air emerged from inside.

"*Hola*," he greeted us.

"*Hola*," we both replied.

"We're interested in the sugar cane juice," I added.

The man nodded and motioned for us to follow him around the main building and across a small muddy stretch to a wall-less shed in the back. Near the front of the open-air space was an antiquated sugar cane press bolted to a concrete block. The squat, sturdy cast-iron device could have been mistaken for a cousin of the potbelly stove. Once a vibrant red, it had faded to the color of a weatherworn brick. "The C.S. Bell Co." and "Hillsboro, Ohio" were emblazoned in raised lettering on the front. Long arms made from white plastic piping extended horizontally from the top of the anachronistic apparatus like a helicopter rotor.

There was a pile of freshly harvested sugar cane stalks lying on a tarp nearby. The man took half a dozen of them and loaded them into the maw at the front of the press. A light blue plastic pitcher was placed next to a spout jutting out the side of it. He took a step back and nodded, pleased with his preparations.

"*Pulsa*," he motioned for me to go over to one of the arms, which was just about shoulder height. Another pipe extended vertically downward, which I grabbed like I was the anchorman in a tug of war.

"I'll be over here if you need any help," my father joked. "Now get to work. I'm thirsty."

210

"Gee, thanks, Dad," I shot back as I began pushing, walking in a wide circle around the press. My feet followed a shallow groove in the dirt floor, a path that had been followed thousands of times. There was a crunchy snapping noise, which seems like a contradiction of terms until you hear sugar cane being pressed. It sounded as if millions of toothpicks suddenly cried out in terror and were suddenly silenced.

The owner of the property seemed satisfied with my contribution after only a few minutes. He held up his hand to bring me to a halt.

"Are you sure you don't want me to keep going?" Dad kidded from the sidelines.

Placing a cheesecloth sieve over a clear glass pitcher, our host poured a stream of pale yellow-green liquid through it. Two matching Tom Collins glasses decorated with circular patterns appeared from somewhere and were each filled to the one-quarter mark.

"*Salud*," my father offered, and we clinked cups.

Tipping back the glass, I took a sip. The juice was just slightly grassy – not unlike a shot of wheatgrass – and definitely sweet though not cloying. I imagined it would pair perfectly with a spritz of fresh lime or a splash of pineapple juice. Of course, Dad had other ideas.

"Does this go well with rum?" he asked, jiggling his glass from side to side.

The sugar cane farmer smiled. "*Uno momento.*" He headed back to the main building and reappeared a moment later with a secondhand bottle filled with a clear liquid. *That looks all too much like the bathtub booze Dad tried in the Azores*, I thought to myself, which got me wondering how you said "designated driver" in Spanish.

"Is that made with sugar cane?" I inquired, trying not to sound too wary.

Our host nodded. *"Guaro."*

He pulled out a small egg cup in the shape of a hen, which looked much more manageably sized than the Azorean glassware. He poured a little of his Costa Rican firewater into it and handed it to my father.

Dad slugged it back quickly and handed the glass back to our host, who graciously poured me a tipple. I tried to toss it into the back of my throat to keep the DIY alcohol off my palate as much as possible. Not that there was much to taste. The cane spirits burned like homemade moonshine, but there was no detectable sugary flavor. Actually, it wasn't that bad. It would certainly take the edge off a long, hard day working in the fields.

I don't know whether it was the alcohol or the sugar rush, but my father was in high spirits when we got back in the car. My mood matched his.

"That was something else, wasn't it?" he remarked as he fastened his seatbelt. "You don't get to experience something like that every day."

"Definitely not," I agreed. At moments like this, I realized that my father and I were more similar than I would have recognized or acknowledged when I was growing up. We both loved adventuring, craved a life less ordinary, and were willing to try something new – at least once – if only to say we had done it.

The drive to Monteverde continued for two more hours, our journey forward getting sharper and more treacherous at every twist and turn. At times we would have to circumvent fallen trees or avoid gaping holes where the roadway had been washed away by mudslides. Sometimes we drove at a snail's pace, and even on the clearest straightaways we topped out at only 20 miles per hour.

We finally pulled into the outback town of Santa Elena at the heart of the Monteverde region in the middle of the day. With an abundance of Internet cafés, gift shops, and tour companies offering zip-lining excursions and nature hikes, it seemed like a modern-day metropolis compared to previous ports of call like

Puerto Ayacucho, Venezuela, and Salelologa, Savai'i.

"Looks pretty touristy," my father noted as we drove along the main thoroughfare to the far edge of the bustling burg where I remembered going to Café Monteverde for double espressos. I didn't want him fixating on the downsides of our destination, so I began chattering about my last trip to Costa Rica until we pulled up at the coffee shop. Scratch that. It was the concrete building that used to house the coffee shop. Now it was someplace called Monteverde Wholefoods. Or at least that's what it was going to be called until Whole Foods' lawyers found out about it.

"It used to be right here," I insisted, already feeling defensive about my navigational error though my father hadn't said anything. I got out of the car, hoping to quickly find a correction. "Maybe they can tell us where it moved."

Walking into the not-a-café, I was pleased discover one of the most charming markets I've ever been in. As far as personality and heart went, this place was way better than any Whole Foods back in the States. A low-slung table at the front of the crowded space had a modest selection of local organic produce, there were neatly kept shelves full of gourmet groceries, and fresh-baked goods were piled by the register. I would have been happy to have this place in my D.C. neighborhood – where the closest "market" was a 7-Eleven – never mind out here in the middle of nowhere.

After buying a few edible souvenirs, I inquired after Café Monteverde's well-being. Was it still around? The woman behind the counter had clearly answered this question before. No, it had not gone out business. Yes, I could breathe a deep sigh of relief. It had simply moved into a larger, more modern space on the other side of town.

Before we began the final leg of our journey to the java mecca, we stopped at the CASEM (Cooperative of Artisans of Santa Elena and Monteverde) gift shop and art gallery next door to the market. The backroom had been converted into a small *soda* (cantina), Cuchara de Abuela, which turned out to be another choice find. We had glasses of freshly squeezed mango juice alongside plastic plates brimming with stir-fried rice mixed with caramelized onions, strands of pepper, and scallion rounds. It was easily the best meal of the trip that didn't include fish we had caught.

We tried not to crow about our good fortune too often between bites, but it was hard not to be ebullient. There's nothing better than hitting a lucky streak when you're traveling, especially when it includes great food.

"That was wonderful," my father noted as he scraped up his last forkful. "Who would have thought we could have a meal this good all the way out here?"

I pushed away my own empty plate. "That was impressive."

"And yet so simple," Dad added. "You can't beat the basics done well."

Our stomachs full, we headed across town to finally get what by now was a highly anticipated cup of espresso. We had been in the car for close to five hours – the longest commute either of us had ever made for a caffeine fix.

When we pulled up in front of Café Monteverde, I had another moment of doubt. There was a proper parking lot outside filled with jeeps and SUVs. The store was now located in a little strip mall, and there was a professionally printed sign in the window. It didn't seem as fetching and homespun as I had remembered it. Well, there was no going back now.

The café was almost deserted, except for the barista behind the waist-high counter who was making a latte to go. I say barista because he didn't have the air of someone who simply worked in a coffee shop as a way to make a few bucks. No, this guy clearly took his coffee seriously. He packed his espresso pucks with focus, kept his equipment spotless, and was ready with nuanced tasting notes when I asked about the various beans they had available.

"That one has a deep, toasted-cacao flavor," he noted when I asked about a bag of oil-rich dark roast beans redolent with a swoon-worthy mocha aroma. "But it's got quite a creamy texture."

As I piled over a dozen bags of coffee on the counter to take home for my personal indulgence and as gifts, this backwoods barista pulled us a pair of double espressos. My father's face lit up like he had just scratched off a winning lottery ticket.

"Look at that froth," he exclaimed. "Perfect."

There was no lemon twist on the side, but my father was too busy shoveling three generous spoons' worth of refined cane sugar into his cup to notice. We sat down at a square table that was designed to double as a shallow shadow box. Underneath a thick plastic top, there were two triangular savannas of coffee beans – one roasted nearly black and the other a robust mahogany.

I waited for my father to try his espresso first, my fingers mentally crossed. He daintily tipped back the small white cup and took a sip. He paused for a moment then replaced the cup in the saucer. I didn't breathe.

"That is one of the best cups of espresso I've ever had," he said, reaching down to go back for a second taste almost as if he didn't believe what he was saying.

I tried not to let the air whoosh out of my lungs too loudly.

"I'm so glad to hear that," I told him before I finally allowed myself to enjoy my own.

That single cup of espresso became a talking point for my father for the rest of the trip and long after we got home.

"God, it was good," he'd reminisce. "There was just something special about it."

"No doubt about that," I'd always reply. "It was unforgettable."

* * * * *

We had one more day open in our schedule before our big fishing expedition on Lago de Cote. Despite my extensive pre-departure research, I was at a loss for how we were going to spend the time.

215

While we were breakfasting at Tom's Pan German Bakery, I desperately leafed through the guidebook looking for an appropriate activity, but nothing seemed right. We had visited Tabacón hot springs when we first arrived, a horseback tour wouldn't do any favors for either of our spines, and white-water rafting seemed a little too vigorous for an 85-year-old.

As a joke, I threw out one outlandish possibility. "We could go zip lining."

"Let's do it," my dad responded coolly, as if he were agreeing to do something that didn't require signing several insurance waivers.

I was a little taken aback. "Are you sure?"

"Why not? I bet it'll be fun."

I could imagine a lot of scenarios where such a situation wouldn't be fun: Dad throwing his back out, somehow falling out of his harness, and plunging to his death in the jungle below or getting stuck in the middle of the line and having an extreme bout of vertigo. However, since I had suggested it – however facetiously – I couldn't back out of the idea. Indira and I had gone zip lining on Kauai a few years earlier and loved it, but we weren't 85-year-old retirees with failing eyesight, a history of heart problems, and prone to the occasional panic attack.

It was a cold, gray day as we retraced the route along the shoreline of Lake Arenal we had taken the day before. However, we took a left turn eastward to the town of Fortuna instead of proceeding south again to the cloud forest. As we got closer, rain started coming down – first in a sprinkle then in a monsoon-worthy downpour.

"I hope we can still go," my father forlornly noted from the passenger seat. "I'm not sure when I'll have a chance to zip line again."

Unfortunately, our lucky streak was broken.

"I'm sorry, but the last group of the day is just finishing up," the

216

cashier told us while we huddled under the awning in front of the ticket window. "No one else can go out on the course in this weather."

He shrugged apologetically. "Our insurance company won't let us run tours in heavy rain."

That sounded reasonable to me, but my father was deeply disappointed at this turn of events. Frankly, so was I. The pictures alone would have been priceless.

"What are we going to do now?" Dad wanted to know.

I didn't have an answer. Here we were, a couple of hours from our lodgings, the rain coming down too hard to do anything outdoors, and no plan of action. I felt like it was my fault and therefore my responsibility to rectify the situation.

I had a single suggestion, but it wasn't one I would have made if there were any other options. A few miles before we had turned off the main road, I noticed a sign for the Arenal Eco Zoo, which boasted a serpentarium, butterfly garden, and frog exhibit. Normally, I would have passed it by and branded it as tourist tripe, but this was not a normal situation.

"It could be interesting," I told my father as I guided the car onward to our new destination, though I didn't believe my own hype. "When she was younger, Jo would definitely have wanted to check it out."

It took us over half an hour to get there, and we didn't talk much on the way. When we arrived, what little hope I was desperately harboring completely abandoned me. The zoo turned out to be a rusticated two-story building that was completely devoid of visitors. In fact, there were only two staff members on hand, including an outgoing teenager who offered to give us the grand tour.

My heart sank. Having come too far to turn back and having no other alternatives on hand, we paid the admission fee and steeled ourselves for a trip to dullsville.

Our first stop was the spider room. Most of the eight-legged mini monsters were neatly pinned down next to typewritten identification tags, but there was a fist-sized tarantula roaming through one terrarium.

"Is it poisonous?" my father wanted to know as he bent down to peer intently at the hairy creature.

"Only if it bites you," our guide joked, "so don't put your hands in the case."

"Reminds me of one of my ex-girlfriends," Dad replied as we moved on to the next section of the zoo, where we were actively encouraged to touch the specimens.

I was handed a red-eyed green tree frog, which settled into the palm of my hand like a sultan going for a ride in his royal palanquin. My father was given a small harlequin green lizard, which quickly skittered up his arm, across his shoulders, and up into his mop of white hair. After a momentary survey of his surroundings, he took a flying leap from my father's head to mine.

Dad quickly snapped a picture of my new tenant. "I think he likes you."

"I like him, too," I replied. "As long as he doesn't pee on me."

Later in the tour, we both got to handle a six-foot-long python. My father wound it around his neck and pretended to be strangled while the snake did its best to pretend like it hadn't been transformed from a fearsome predator into a dubious fashion accessory. I took a quick snapshot of my father grasping the reptile like a hangman's noose while bugging out his eyes and lolling his tongue.

"This should be your Christmas card," I told him, which earned a chuckle.

The rest of the tour proved to be equally engaging. We examined the inner workings of see-through frogs, heard stories about venomous fer-de-lance snakes – which always ended poorly for the

218

humans who encountered them – and caught a pair of turtles rutting during a mid-morning swim. When all was said and done, we spent nearly two hours at the museum. I'm sure it was a new record for time spent indoors at a tourist attraction on a family vacation.

"That was actually really cool," I told my father as we hit the road back to our rental property.

"It was," he agreed.

We both sounded a little surprised but very pleased. As I piloted us homeward along the jungle highway, a comfortable silence settled over us, as if all our energy in the car had found some new equilibrium.

* * * * *

When we woke early the next morning, the weather hadn't improved. Rain was lashing against the windows, a thick blanket of mist clung to the jungle, and the temperature was cold enough to require long sleeves and pants.

"I hope we can still go fishing," my father said as we nursed steaming cups of rich Costa Rican coffee sweetened with dark cane sugar. "I'd hate to have come all this way for nothing."

A short while later, we were standing in Jim Harvey's slate-paved living room. In front of the fireplace stood an artificial Christmas tree covered in lights and sentimental decorations that recalled a snowier holiday season. Our guide sported a gray-and-white goatee, well-worn hands, and a sun-wrinkled face.

"This is nothing," he told us when I worried aloud that the weather would scuttle our plans. "We'll catch a lot."

When I asked why more people didn't go to Lago de Cote if the fishing was so good, he gestured toward a black-and-white aerial photograph hanging on the wall.

"Most people come here because of the flying saucer," he said.

Taken in 1971 by a mapping crew from the Costa Rican National Geographic Institute at 10,000 feet, the picture clearly captures a slightly peaked disk hovering above the lake. UFO enthusiasts continue to debate its validity online and frequently make pilgrimages to the lake in hopes of making further sightings. Neither Jim nor his wife, Debra, had ever seen anything out of the ordinary, other than the ufologists who occasionally showed up unannounced.

After hitching his small boat to the back of his battered Land Rover, we rumbled down the muddy road, which was often just water-filled tire ruts running side by side, to the lake. The scene reinforced my growing sense that we were on the set of *The X-Files*. There was no defined shoreline; instead, the edge of the lake indiscriminately flooded the fields and forests surrounding it. Trees devoured by the advancing waters jutted out of the dark lake like hands grasping in supplication.

The fog was so thick that I couldn't see the far side, even though the lake is only about two-thirds of a mile wide and covers just under 1.25 square miles. As the boat chugged across the white-tipped waters, we huddled beneath its meager awning to avoid the worst of the rain. To help ward off the damp, Jim poured us shots of *guaro*, which looked like it had a more commercial provenance than the stuff we had tried the day before.

On the far side of the lake, near a pair of giant sunken trees, we let our lured lines fly for the first time. Given the depressing weather and the surreal surroundings, my hopes weren't high. The boat hadn't glided 20 feet, however, before my father's pole bowed toward the water.

"It's a hit!" he yelled as he reeled in. This time, there wasn't a throwback on the end but a three-pound machaca. Minutes later, he was repeating his performance. He made it a hat trick within the first half-hour. Holding up his third catch, he flashed a smile that took decades off his face.

Despite the foul weather, he took a seat up at the exposed front of the boat. Bundled up in a salamander orange windbreaker, tan rain pants, and a long-billed hat with a back flap to keep the nonexistent sunshine off his neck, he stood out against the dreamlike surroundings.

A moment later he was triumphantly crowing, "Another one!"

I wasn't doing too badly either, having pulled up a pair of decent-size *machaca*. We would feast tonight.

I could already imagine the stories he was going to tell about this expedition. Our catch would be multiplied, the bad weather amplified, and the oddity of our surroundings exaggerated.

And I would never contradict his version of events, even though, for me, the simple fact that we were spending time together was the perfect story.

We had worked a lifetime to get to this moment. As we grew older, we both got mellower in our own ways. For Dad, that meant relinquishing some of the control he wielded when I was younger, while I learned to be more forgiving and understanding of his choices.

Seeing him that happy that morning on Lago de Cote and sharing that joy was more than worth every death-defying plane ride, losing my breakfast in the South Pacific, failing as an owl hunter, being ordered into piranha-infested waters for a bottle of scotch, and getting food poisoning combined. Looking back, I saw all those moments for what they really were – adventures.

Epilogue

I was standing at the center of a small island, its tiny acreage overrun with brightly dressed pygmies. They were dashing to and fro at high speeds, uttering ecstatic cries, and flailing their arms and legs though it wasn't always clear why. Every few moments, one would run pell-mell straight toward me. I would move to get out of the way, but often the short figure would inexplicably change direction before we came close to colliding, like a pinball ricocheting off an invisible flipper.

Before me, a fantastical two-story structure stretched up toward the sky. Like a tree fort without a leafy perch, the green-and-brown-toned framework looked as if Peter Pan and a few Ewoks had designed it after eating their body weight in acid. Spires jutted out at odd angles, Escher-esque steps led to oddly shaped appendages, and a rainbow of thick plastic tubes wrapped around the exterior like Technicolor ribs.

The noisy mob of tiny humanoids swarmed through its every nook and cranny, an army of ants overcoming an ice cream cone dropped on the sidewalk. Part of me wanted to explore this bizarre building with them, but I didn't want to violate any unspoken tribal rules or accidentally upset any ancient rites. My wife, Indira, stood next to me, on high alert as she intently surveyed the joyful mayhem.

A lifetime of living strange on the far side of the far side suddenly seemed quite normal. Forget land-diving rituals, kava ceremonies, and fishing for *machaca* at a UFO landing site, my new adventures as a parent outshined any of my previous escapades.

My reverie was broken as our one-year-old son barreled by, leaning into his run so that his head was in front of his feet. His arms stretched out straight behind him like an Olympic ski jumper in midair. The fin on his shark-shaped hat bobbed up and down with each step, turning him into a miniature Jaws pursuing a school full of kaleidoscopically colored fish. He looked neither left nor right; his eyes were locked on some point on the other side of this Seuss-worthy islet.

"Be careful, Zephyr," I called after him.

He probably didn't even realize we were there. I moved to follow him across the playground, keeping my distance but still close enough that I could swoop in and intervene to prevent him from injuring himself or others.

"Keep an eye on him," Indira told me before adding, "Poppa."

I had to smile. Now I was the dad and my father was Grandpa. He never did move to Costa Rica.

"Don't worry," I called over my shoulder without shifting my focus from our son. "I've got him covered."

Having my own family to take care of made me realize something that all my years of travel did not. Home is not a place – it's a feeling, a sense of belonging, the freedom to be yourself, comfort in the darkest hours, unstoppable joy. Home is your favorite album, book, and movie all rolled into one. It's familiar but always new. When you find home, there's nowhere else you'd rather be. Perhaps the best thing is that you can carry it with you. Suddenly, the world is your home.

Both my parents instilled in me a deep desire for discovery. They taught me to seek out the unusual, remain open to unexpected opportunities, try new foods, and be friendly to everyone. My mother worked hard to give me a sense of security and teach me how to conduct myself gracefully in the family dynamic. On the other hand, my father taught me to value a good espresso, ditch the guidebook occasionally, and always wear a bathing suit to the beach.

Those experiences and the confidence of my home with Indira and Zephyr – wherever that may be – make me excited to show my new family the far corners of the globe, albeit with more insistence on seatbelts, airbags, and life jackets.

So far, my young family has only breezed around America together, but international trips loom on the horizon – my wife's homeland of Ghana, Iceland, Easter Island, Thailand, and Morocco all hover near the top of our bucket list.

Zephyr seems ready to discover the world with us, refusing to sit still for long. Sometimes he'll go somewhere he shouldn't, start pounding something that's too delicate, or try eating something that wasn't designed to be digested. Indira and I will lunge across the room to stop him, usually wreaking more havoc in the process.

No matter how far up the creek we are at that moment and no matter what is hitting the fan, I have to laugh. This is my new freak show. Let the adventures begin.

> **"We shall not cease from exploration**
> **And the end of all our exploring**
> **Will be to arrive where we started**
> **And know the place for the first time."**
>
> **T.S. Eliot, "Little Gidding"**

Acknowledgments

My first acknowledgment goes to my editor and publisher, Meredith Maslich, who saw my vision for the book and helped me get it right on the page. Thank you for believing in this freak show.

Benedictions to those who read this manuscript and gave me much-needed editorial feedback: Kelly "You. Are. A. Fucking. Genius." DiNardo, Rachel Kaufman, Shelby Reynolds, Kate Parham, and Jenny Rough.

So many thanks to Carrie Hamilton for her beautiful cover design. If you're ever in the market for an incredibly talented and thoughtful designer, you can find her online at kismetdesign.com. My gratitude goes out to Sam Dulik for his translation work. I have endless praise for primo publicists Charissa Benjamin and Elaine Mazanec of Savor PR for all their hard work, creative thinking, and upbeat attitudes. And let's give a standing ovation to director Ken "Wessence" Cornwell, editor extraordinaire Alex Johnson, Kyle "Young Nevin" Ensley and Katia Kianpour for the wonderful book trailer. Bravo, bravo!

Family is everything to me, so I'd like to give a shout-out to my original freak show: Mom, Dad, and Jo. Thank you for all that you've done and all that you are. The tree has grown more branches, so love goes out to Will, Flossie, Gus, Phin, Maribeth, Big O and Mummy, Yao, Yom, Jared, Poppy and her new brother, the ever-expanding Murray clan, the Spiegels, the Werners, and the Labor Day crew.

I need to extend a big thanks to my current and former editors, who have helped me become a better writer. This includes Pat McGuire, Patrick Strange, Mikel Jollett, Joe Yonan, Bonnie Benwick, Zofia Smardz, Michael McCarthy, Emili Vesilind, Erin Hartigan, Lisa Shroder, Jennifer Barger, Chris Shott, Liz Grossman, Jenny Sullivan, Katie Bianco, David Barker, Holley Simmons, Clay Beacham, Dria de Botton, Paul Schnee, and everyone else whom I'm forgetting.

A few records were key inspirations – Nightlands' *Oak Island*, Local Natives' *Hummingbird*, and John Newman's *Tribute* – as were the classical stylings of WETA 90.9 FM and the works of Steve Reich. Thanks for being there during the loneliest hours.

Here's a tip of the mug to all the coffee shops and cafés that gave me a place to work while constantly replenishing my brain with caffeine: Capital City Cheesecake, Qualia Coffee, the Coffee Bar, Chinatown Coffee Co., Peregrine, and La Mano Coffee Bar.

Most of all, I want to acknowledge my wife, Indira, and my son, Zephyr. Thank you both for loving and supporting me while I wrestled with this story. You brighten my days, sharpen my mind, make my heart thrum, and create endless joy. I love you.

Photo Credit: Scott Suchman

About the Author

Nevin Martell is a D.C.-based food, travel, and lifestyle writer whose work regularly appears in the *Washington Post, Plate, Wine Enthusiast,* TravelChannel.com and NPR's blog "The Salt." He is the author of five books, including *The Founding Farmers Cookbook: 100 Recipes for True Food & Drink* (2013) and the small-press smash *Looking for Calvin and Hobbes: The Unconventional Story of Bill Watterson and his Revolutionary Comic Strip* (2009). When he can budget the time and money, he loves nothing more than traveling with his wife and son. Find him online at nevinmartell.com and on Twitter @nevinmartell.